FICHTE'S THEORY OF SUBJECTIVITY

FREDERICK NEUHOUSER
Harvard University

The right of the
University of Cambridge
to print and sell
all manner of books
was granted by
Henry VIII in 1534.
The University has printed
and published continuously
since 1584.

CAMBRIDGE UNIVERSITY PRESS
CAMBRIDGE

NEW YORK   PORT CHESTER   MELBOURNE   SYDNEY

Published by the Press Syndicate of the University of Cambridge
The Pitt Building, Trumpington Street, Cambridge CB2 1RP
40 West 20th Street, New York, NY 10011, USA
10 Stamford Road, Oakleigh, Melbourne 3166, Australia

© Cambridge University Press 1990

First published 1990

Library of Congress Cataloging-in-Publication Data
Neuhouser, Frederick.
Fichte's theory of subjectivity / Frederick Neuhouser.
p. cm. – (Modern European philosophy)
Includes bibliographical references.
ISBN 0-521-37433-2. – ISBN 0-521-39938-6 (pbk.)
1. Fichte, Johann Gottlieb, 1762–1814 – Contributions in concept of
subjectivity. 2. Subjectivity. I. Title. II. Series.
B2849.S92N48 1990
126 – dc20
89-49731
CIP

British Library Cataloguing in Publication Data
Neuhouser, Frederick
Fichte's theory of subjectivity. – (Modern European
philosophy).
1. German philosphy. Fichte, Johann Gottlieb
I. Title II. Series
193

ISBN 0-521-37433-2 hardback
ISBN 0-521-39938-6 paperback

Transferred to digital printing 1999

FOR UDAY

CONTENTS

ACKNOWLEDGMENTS

Many people have been of help to me in a variety of ways during my work on this project. Above all, I am indebted to Charles Larmore, whose detailed and thoughtful comments on several drafts have made this a significantly better book than it otherwise would have been. I have also benefited greatly from conversations and correspondence with Daniel Breazeale, Maudemarie Clark, Stephen Engstrom, Raymond Geuss, Michael Hardimon, Pierre Keller, Charles Parsons, Thomas Pogge, and David Weberman. I would like to express my gratitude as well to Robert Pippin, who made his work on Fichte available to me long before it appeared in print, and to Daniel Parish, who prepared the index and spent many hours checking the accuracy of my translations. In addition, I have received generous financial assistance from the Edwin and Louise Bechtel Fund of the Harvard Philosophy Department, as well as a year-long fellowship in 1987–8 from the Mrs. Giles Whiting Foundation, during which time I was able to complete a first draft of the entire manuscript. Special thanks are due to Elisabeth Gladir and Deutsches Haus, Columbia University, who generously allowed me the use of the office space in which most of these pages were written. Finally, I would like to thank Uday Dhar for the encouragement he provided throughout the entire project, without which it surely would not have been completed.

ABBREVIATIONS

GA   *J. G. Fichte: Gesamtausgabe der Bayerischen Akademie der Wissenschaften,* ed. R. Lauth, H. Jacobs, and H. Gliwitsky

GMS   Kant, *Grundlegung zur Metaphysik der Sitten* (*Groundwork of the Metaphysic of Morals*)

KPV   Kant, *Kritik der praktischen Vernunft* (*Critique of Practical Reason*)

KRV   Kant, *Kritik der reinen Vernunft* (*Critique of Pure Reason*)

KU   Kant, *Kritik der Urteilskraft* (*Critique of Judgment*)

SW   *Johann Gottlieb Fichtes sämmtliche Werke,* ed. I. H. Fichte

WL 1794   Fichte, *Die Grundlage der gesammten Wissenschaftslehre* (1794) (*The Science of Knowledge,* trans. P. Heath and J. Lachs)

INTRODUCTION

In 1795, in the first published version of his major philosophical work, Fichte declares that one of the fundamental goals of his thought is to bring "*unity* and *coherence* into the entire human being."[1] In describing his system in these terms, Fichte gives expression to the basic aim that motivates the specific project with which this book is concerned. That project can be characterized as an attempt to construct a "theory of subjectivity," a theory that, to use the term Fichte himself preferred, provides an explanation of what it is to be an "I." Since it is not immediately clear what such a project will involve, or why it is worthy of being undertaken, it will be necessary to say something about the general nature of Fichte's task before we attempt to understand it in full detail. In the first place, we shall need to know what exactly a theory of subjectivity is a theory of. Moreover, what are the philosophical problems that give rise to the need for such a theory? Finally, what role can a theory of subjectivity play in establishing the "unity and coherence" of the human being?

Let us begin with the most basic question of all: What *is* a theory of subjectivity? Or, more precisely, what is it that *Fichte's*

---

1. "Es kommt durch dieses System *Einheit* und *Zusammenhang* in den ganzen Menschen," SW, I, p. 295.

1

theory of the subject aims to accomplish? As Fichte conceives of it, the basic goal of his theory is to develop an account of the essential nature of subjecthood, or to provide an explanation of what it is that makes a subject a subject. Part of this undertaking will consist in articulating the important ways in which subjects are distinct from nonsubjects or, in other words, in giving an answer to the question "How is a subject different from a thing?" Central to this task will be the search for a principle that defines what it is to be a subject in a way similar to that in which the notions of 'substance' and 'causal determination' define the constitutive features of objects. But grasping the essential nature of subjectivity will involve more than comprehending the differences between an I and a not-I; it should, on Fichte's view, also enable us to understand how the various capacities we ascribe to subjects can be viewed as grounded in, or made possible by, the unique set of properties that are said to constitute the subject's essential nature. In other words, Fichte will strive to achieve a *unified* account of subjectivity, one attempting to explain the apparently diverse activities of the subject in terms of a single structure that underlies and informs them all. Most important to us here will be Fichte's attempt to unify the theoretical and practical aspects of subjectivity by showing that the capacities for knowledge and free agency both depend upon one distinctive, "subjective" feature of the I. When formulated in this way, it becomes clear that Fichte's theory can be understood as a contribution to the classical philosophical debate concerning the relation between theory and practice; or, to express it in Kantian terms, Fichte attempts to comprehend the relation between theoretical and practical reason. The search to find a single structure of subjectivity, then, will be intimately related to the question as to whether reason itself is of a unitary nature and, if so, how that nature is to be conceived.

A significant portion of this study will be devoted to filling in the details of the general project just outlined. In doing so, we shall attempt to understand how Fichte arrived at this particular conception of what a theory of subjectivity should be, as well as why he came to regard such a theory as the primary concern of philosophy. It is only after retracing this rather complex set of developments that we shall be in a position to comprehend the factors that led Fichte to construct his theory of subjectivity as he did. Yet even before we have examined this history in detail, it is possible to get a rough idea of the problem that his theory, at its most fundamental level, is intended to address. As we shall see in

much greater detail later, Fichte's inquiry into the nature of the
subject is motivated primarily by concerns relating to the *practical*
aspect of subjectivity, and especially to questions concerning the
intelligibility of human freedom, or 'self-determination'. In order
to understand the nature of these concerns, as well as the significance of Fichte's response to them, it will be necessary to recall
briefly the historical context within which they arose.

The feature of the contemporary philosophical landscape that
is of greatest importance for our purposes is directly connected
to the rise of a form of Spinozism in Germany during the latter
half of the eighteenth century. The particular version of Spinozism
that is relevant here was articulated most compellingly by F. H.
Jacobi in his popular book *Letters on the Doctrine of Spinoza,* which
was first published in 1785.[2] The most important aspect of
Jacobi's interpretation of Spinoza was his formulation and defense
of the claim that the belief in human freedom is incompatible with
the view of reality that reason seems to require us to accept.
Jacobi's claim is not merely that the belief in our own freedom
cannot be rationally justified; he holds that any thoroughly consistent, rational understanding of the world will be committed to
ruling out this very possibility. We are forced, then, on Jacobi's
view, to choose between an irrational faith in the possibility of
freedom and a rational but completely deterministic view of the
world in which there is no room for self-determined agency. One
consequence of Jacobi's claim that will play a significant role in
our discussion of Fichte's early development concerns the implications of such a claim for the possibility of morality. If reason
cannot be reconciled with the belief in our own freedom, then it is
just as incompatible with the idea that human beings are bound
by moral duties. Since attributing moral obligation to an agent
seems to require that the agent be free to do her duty or not, a
world without freedom would also be one in which there could be
no moral "ought." A commitment to reason, it would seem,
implies that we must also regard commonsense beliefs in both
freedom and morality as mere illusions.

It is important to note that the plausibility of Jacobi's view
depends upon a particular conception of the nature of rationality –
a conception that finds its classical formulation in the principle of

---

2. A more detailed account of the controversy surrounding Spinoza and the effect
   it had on subsequent German philosophy is given by Beiser (1987). See especially Chap. 2, pp. 44–91.

sufficient reason. According to this principle (or at least the version of it that is relevant here), every existing state of affairs Y is grounded in some other set of conditions X such that the presence of X is sufficient to necessitate the existence of Y. The troubling implication of this view is easily seen: How is it possible to conceive of the human being as capable of free action, if his deeds are all necessary consequences of prior conditions external to himself? In one of his earliest published writings Fichte struggles to find a solution to this very problem, which he formulates in the following way:[3] If it is necessary to posit a sufficient reason, or "ground" (*Grund*), for every event, then such a ground must be thought to exist for all of the will's choices as well. But if we can in principle always find a reason to explain the will's choice of a particular action, we are also capable of showing that the action in question *had* to be chosen and that its opposite was rejected with equal necessity. In this case, however, it is also shown that the will did not make a free, undetermined choice at all. In other words, if the principle of sufficient reason holds universally, then it must apply even to determinations of the will, but the existence of this kind of ground for the will's actions seems to be incompatible with the undetermined choice necessary for a conception of human freedom.

Although the details of Fichte's earliest attempts to solve this problem are too complex to concern us here, it is easy to see that his basic strategy must involve, in some form, a denial of the universal applicability of the principle of sufficient reason. The main advantage of such a move is obvious enough: If the principle of sufficient reason is no longer claimed to hold for all of reality, then no special problem is posed by regarding some events, such as the will's choices, as free from causal determination.

The idea of denying universal validity to this principle of reason does not, of course, originate with Fichte. Kant's own distinction between appearances and things in themselves, along with his restriction of the principle of causality to the former, can be understood as one rather elaborate version of this strategy. Unfortunately, limiting the applicability of the principle of sufficient reason gives rise to a whole new set of serious difficulties. The various problems engendered by Kant's distinction between the

---

3. The work in question is the so-called Creuzer review (GA, I.2, pp. 7–14; SW, VIII, pp. 411–17), which is discussed in greater detail in Chapters 1 and 4.

noumenal and phenomenal realms are well known, and we shall have occasion to examine one of them in greater detail in Chapter 1. For now it will be sufficient to point out the one issue that is most relevant to understanding the basic motivation behind Fichte's theory of subjectivity: If we exempt the will's actions from the kind of rational explanations provided by the principle of sufficient reason, what conception of these actions and their agents are we left with?

In my opinion, the answer to this question constitutes the implicit starting point for all of Fichte's subsequent thinking about the subject: As long as the only notion of reason available to us is the one embodied in the principle of sufficient reason, rationality must appear as completely irrelevant and alien to the exercise of freedom. Why, though, should we find this disturbing? First, such a view seems to allow no way of understanding free actions other than as random occurrences. The agents of these actions may indeed be undetermined by external causes, but are they free in any sense that matters to us – that is, are they really *self-*determined? If freedom were to consist in mere randomness, it would be unclear why being free would bestow a higher worth upon human agents than that possessed by causally determined things. Second, in simply denying the applicability of the principle of sufficient reason to the will's choices, we not only rule out the possibility of giving a causal explanation of free acts, we also make it impossible to explain or to understand those acts in any sense whatsoever. We are left, in other words, with another version of the dilemma referred to earlier: If we deny that our free acts can be explained by something like the principle of sufficient reason, we seem to have no choice other than to espouse a wholly inscrutable kind of freedom, one that precludes any kind of rational understanding of free acts, including the actions of others as well as our own. Rejecting the principle of sufficient reason may succeed in salvaging a kind of freedom, but it does so only at the expense of our self-comprehension as free agents.

The upshot of these considerations is that a satisfactory response to the challenge of Jacobi's Spinoza requires more than a simple denial of the universal validity of the principle of sufficient reason. What is also needed is an alternative account of reason, one that makes it possible to understand freedom as a kind of self-determination and that is able to conceive of actions as grounded in reasons without at the same time making them into externally determined, unfree events. Kant's moral philosophy – and especially his articulation of a "practical" form of reason – can be understood as an attempt to carry out precisely this task. It is not surprising, then, that Fichte's own philosophical career began with an appropriation of the doctrines of Critical Philosophy. Since the considerations that ultimately led Fichte beyond Kant's position are too complex to treat adequately in this introduction, we shall postpone a detailed examination of them until Chapters 1 and 2. For the present it is sufficient simply to note that the most important way in which Fichte's own theory of subjectivity aimed to improve upon Kant's was by providing a *unitary* account of the subject, one that would bring "unity and coherence into the human being" by showing that there are not two distinct faculties of reason but, at root, only one. His task, then, takes the form of a search to discover the single principle that governs the entire realm of subjectivity – a principle that defines what it is to be a subject in a theoretical as well as a practical sense and that, by so doing, both explains the possibility and illuminates the nature of rational self-determination. As we shall see, one consequence of his quest for a unitary theory of subjectivity is that Fichte is ultimately led toward a conception of self-determination that diverges in fundamental ways from Kant's own notion of moral autonomy but that is relevant to still unresolved questions concerning the nature of human freedom. By reconstructing the content of Fichte's theory and the history of its development, I hope to show that, despite its often bewildering obscurity, Fichte's thought contains a number of insights powerful enough to have opened up an inquiry into the nature of subjectivity that, even today, has not been brought to completion.

The interpretation I present here ought not to be regarded as an attempt to write the final word on Fichte. Rather, it represents what I hope will be a contribution to a continuing discussion of both Fichte's philosophy and the foundations of German Idealism in general. As such, its ambitions are limited in a number of significant respects that perhaps should be made explicit at the outset. In treating Fichte's philosophy as, above all else, a "theory of subjectivity," I aim to give a somewhat more systematic account of his position than could be had by focusing upon one particular aspect of his thought and examining it in isolation from his broader systematic goals. At the same time, however, my attempt to deal with a central issue in a systematic way clearly falls short of providing a comprehensive account of Fichte's thought as a whole. There are, by necessity, many interesting and important aspects of his philosophical system that are simply left untreated here.

A further limitation of my interpretation is that it restricts itself to the early portion of Fichte's philosophical career, a period I define as extending from 1790, the time of his earliest unpublished writings, to approximately 1799. Although, as we shall see in Chapter 2, Fichte's views underwent rapid and fundamental changes even within this period, the year 1799 marks a natural breaking point in his lifelong development. By this time Fichte had already finished the first complete version of his philosophical system, which, in addition to his more widely known *Wissenschafts-lehre* (of which there are a number of different versions already within this early period), includes two other major works, *System of the Doctrine of Morals* (1798) as well as a treatise on political theory, *Foundation of Natural Right* (1796). More importantly, it was in 1799 that Fichte found himself embroiled in a vicious public debate over the alleged atheistic implications of his own philosophical views.[4] This so-called Atheism Controversy eventually led to Fichte's dismissal from his position at the University of Jena, but its consequences extended beyond his change of residence to Berlin. For after 1800 Fichte's thought is based upon a fundamentally new conception of his system, one that is not only obscure in the typically Fichtean manner, but also extremely difficult to understand as a continuous development of his earlier views.

Two other considerations influenced my decision to deal only with those of Fichte's works written before 1800. First, the early texts played a far more significant role than his later ones in shaping the course German philosophy was to take after Kant. Although both Hegel and Schelling were still philosophically active well into the first three decades of the nineteenth century, it was Fichte's thought before 1800 that had the greatest effect on the development of their own philosophical systems. With the exception of two of his popular works, *The Vocation of Man* (1800) and *Addresses to the German Nation* (1808), Fichte's later writings failed, for the most part, to exert a significant influence on subsequent

4. An account of the Atheism Controversy is provided by Breazeale in Fichte (1988, pp. 40–5).

philosophy. Second, Fichte's early thought is closest, both chronologically and in terms of content, to the philosophy of Kant. This
is important because it is here, if anywhere, that we should begin
in order to comprehend the complicated historical development
that leads from Kant's Critical Philosophy to nineteenth-century
Idealism. Moreover, if we are ever to achieve a more adequate
understanding of Fichte's thought as a whole, we shall need to
begin with his earliest system. This is not merely a matter of proceeding chronologically. Rather, it is necessitated by the fact that
Fichte's most important texts are virtually incomprehensible if
simply delved into without some external point of reference. It
is my view – and this assumption has guided the writing of this
book – that the only way of making sense of these texts is to begin
by situating them in relation to more familiar philosophical ter-
rain, which in this case must be the philosophy of Kant.

There is at least one more significant respect in which the interpretation I offer here must be regarded as incomplete. A number
of prominent claims made by Fichte are relevant to the topics of
this book but receive little attention in my account of his theory
of subjectivity. This is perhaps most true of my treatment of
Fichte's practical philosophy. As I explain in Chapter 4, the conception of self-determination that I emphasize here is not the
notion most visible in his texts – that of moral autonomy in the
Kantian sense – but one that, though clearly present, is suggested
rather than fully elaborated by Fichte himself. Moreover, my
account of the relationship between theoretical and practical subjectivity gives short shrift to one of the positions that is most
widely associated with Fichte, the *primacy* of practical over theoretical reason. It is clear from a variety of texts that Fichte did in
fact want to assert, in some form, the primacy of practical reason;
it is less apparent to me that he ever found a plausible way of
understanding that doctrine. Although this claim of Fichte's is
provocative and even historically influential, I do not believe that
it is developed in an illuminating way within his own texts. This
may simply mean that I have been unable to summon the philosophical imagination required to grasp this aspect of his position;
if so, perhaps future interpreters will be able to make more sense
of this doctrine than I. Of course, to emphasize, as I do, Fichte's
views concerning the *unity* of theoretical and practical reason is
not to rule out that a relation of primacy could also hold between
the two; nevertheless, I do not explore this possibility here. In

short, my decision to emphasize certain aspects of Fichte's views over others was made in light of my principal aim in this book, which is to present a relatively systematic account of Fichte's basic project that is both coherent and philosophically interesting, and that remains true to what I take to be the most fundamental concerns that motivate his thought as a whole.

This book is divided roughly into two halves, each of which is made up of two chapters. The first half is primarily historical in nature and attempts to understand the route by which Fichte arrived at his conception of a theory of subjectivity. Chapter 1 is concerned primarily with an analysis of the notion of the unity of reason. It aims to lay out and distinguish the three most prominent senses in which the post-Kantian project of unifying theoretical and practical reason can be understood. In order to understand the motivation for carrying out such a project, this chapter discusses the young Fichte's dissatisfaction with the two separate accounts of reason given by Kant in the first and second *Critiques*. It also analyzes the relationship between the issue of the unity of reason and what Fichte takes to be another crucial problem in Kant's moral philosophy, the lack of a positive proof that pure reason has a *practical* capacity. Chapter 2 traces Fichte's development from his early criticisms of Kant through the *Wissenschaftslehre* of 1797–9 and examines the various strategies he considers in his attempt to demonstrate the unity of reason. The main concern here is to clarify the sense in which Fichte ultimately comes to regard theoretical and practical subjectivity as unitary. It is argued that his main strategy consists in showing that a single structure underlies consciousness in both its theoretical and practical forms, a structure that he intends to capture with his distinctive notion of the subject's "self-positing" activity.

The second half of the book attempts to reconstruct the details of Fichte's main thesis through separate analyses of the fundamental phenomena of the theoretical and practical realms (Chapters 3 and 4, respectively). Chapter 3 discusses Fichte's conception of the self-positing subject as it is developed in relation to the phenomenon of theoretical self-consciousness. It focuses on three claims about the I's self-awareness that are central to Fichte's view of the subject: the nonrepresentational nature of self-awareness; the role of self-consciousness in securing the unity of consciousness and thereby "grounding" experience; and the self-constituting nature of the subject. Chapter 4 begins by analyzing in some detail the various notions of self-determination that are present in Fichte's ethical theory. Its main intent is to determine how Fichte uses the conception of the self-positing subject developed in the previous chapter to construct a theory of practical self-determination that explains the autonomous subject's relation to itself without recourse to a "two-worlds" view in which the subject of experience is determined by a rational but unknowable noumenal self. The book ends with a brief assessment of the extent to which Fichte's theory succeeds in showing that an identical structure informs both theoretical and practical subjectivity.

Finally, a word about textual sources: Fichte's works appear in German in two excellent sets of collected works: *Johann Gottlieb Fichtes sämmtliche Werke* (SW), edited by Fichte's son, I. H. Fichte, and the more authoritative but still incomplete *J. G. Fichte: Gesamtausgabe der Bayerischen Akademie der Wissenschaften* (GA), edited under the direction of Reinhard Lauth. In the following, initial references to works that appear in both of these collections give page numbers from both editions; subsequent footnotes, however, refer only to the pagination of SW, since these page numbers are also clearly provided in GA. Most of the translations of German sources are my own, although some are based upon the existing English translations cited in the footnotes and bibliography. The most notable exceptions to this generalization are quotations from the *Critique of Pure Reason,* all of which are from Norman Kemp Smith's excellent translation, sometimes with very minor emendations of my own. I have tried to avoid the extensive use of abbreviations in the text; those that I have used for frequently cited sources are listed on page x.

ORIGINS OF FICHTE'S THEORY: THE NOTION OF THE UNITY OF REASON

The first half of our account of Fichte's theory of subjectivity will be devoted primarily to clarifying the basic nature of his project: What precisely is it that Fichte's theory intends to show, and why does he come to regard the development of such a theory as the central task of philosophy? In the first two chapters we shall attempt to answer these questions by examining the historical origins of Fichte's project and by tracing the developments his conception of that project underwent during the early portion of his career. On the basis of what we already know about the general nature of Fichte's theory, the basic issue that will concern us in Chapters 1 and 2 can be formulated as the following question: What reasons might there be for wanting to demonstrate that a single fundamental structure underlies all forms of subjectivity?

As I indicated in the Introduction, the main problem addressed by Fichte has its roots in questions raised by Kant's successors, and to a lesser extent by Kant himself, concerning the relationship between theoretical and practical reason. The question, more precisely, is whether theoretical and practical reason can be said to constitute a single faculty, or whether they must be regarded as essentially heterogeneous. It is, of course, widely recognized that the issue of the unity of reason becomes one of the principal themes of German Idealism after Kant. The need to demonstrate this unity is usually understood as arising from the fact that Kant bequeathed to his followers two distinct accounts of reason, in two separate critiques, but failed to bring these together into a single, unitary theory of the faculty of reason in its most general form. What is often left unarticulated, however, is precisely what kind of unity theoretical and practical reason should be shown to possess and, more importantly, why Kant's inability to do so should be construed as a defect that needs to be remedied. The present chapter aims to give an answer to just these questions and has, therefore, two primary goals. The first of these is to distinguish and discuss three senses in which one might conceive of the "unity" of theoretical and practical reason within the context of Kant's Critical Philosophy. The second is to specify the particular forms that the task of unifying theoretical and practical reason takes in Fichte's earliest, presystematic writings. An important part of the latter goal will be to understand Fichte's motivation for placing the theme of the unity of reason at the center of his philosophical project. In other words, we shall want to know not only in what sense Fichte wanted to uphold the unity of reason but also why he felt so keenly the need to espouse such a position.

Let us begin by specifying the three different senses that the notion of the unity of reason assumes in Fichte's thought. Theoretical and practical reason can be claimed to be unified insofar as

1. they are *compatible* with each other, that is, insofar as the principles of one do not conflict with those of the other;
2. both can be derived as components of a unitary and complete system of philosophy, which has as its starting point a single first principle;
3. they possess an identical underlying "structure," or constitute what is in essence a single activity of the subject.

In what follows I refer to these distinct theses as

1. the compatibility of theoretical and practical reason;
2. the systematic unity of reason; and
3. the structural identity of theoretical and practical reason.

In the rest of this chapter I shall attempt to clarify each of these senses by examining the forms in which they appear in Fichte's earliest philosophical writings.

The compatibility of theoretical
and practical reason

It was in 1790, four years before the publication of the first version of the *Wissenschaftslehre*, that Fichte undertook for the first time a serious study of the central texts of Kantian philosophy. Although his initial reading of the *Critique of Pure Reason* made little impression upon him, his encounter with the second *Critique* was arguably the most powerful and consequential philosophical experience of his life. The most visible effect of this encounter was Fichte's immediate conversion to Kantianism. In a letter to his friend Friedrich Weißhuhn he writes:

> I live in a new world since having read the *Critique of Practical Reason*. . . . Things I thought could never be proved – the concept of absolute freedom, duty, etc. – have been proved, and I feel all the happier because of it. It is incomprehensible how much power and respect for humanity this system gives us!'

Statements such as these leave no room for doubt as to what aroused Fichte's enthusiasm for Critical Philosophy: Kant's account of practical reason in the second *Critique* seemed to provide the philosophical groundwork upon which the reality of morality and human freedom could be affirmed.

After his initial, unqualified acceptance of Critical Philosophy, the first major problem in Kant's system to attract Fichte's attention was the question of the unity of theoretical and practical reason in the first of the three senses distinguished previously. As I have suggested, this sense of the "unity" of reason is best characterized in terms of the *compatibility* of theoretical and practical reason. What is at issue more specifically is the compatibility of the world views that each form of reason requires us to adopt. Formulated in its most general terms, the question addressed here concerns whether the view of the world that follows from the principles of theoretical reason (a world of natural events that occur in accord with universal causal laws) can be reconciled with the kind of world required by the laws of practical reason. As we shall see, this question can be understood in at least two distinct

1. GA, III.1, p. 167.

senses, each of which receives its own treatment at different places in the Kantian system – in the third antinomy of the *Critique of Pure Reason* and in the introduction to the *Critique of Judgment.*

Fichte's concern with the compatibility of theoretical and practical reason is evidenced by a very early unpublished text from the year 1790 that bears the provisional title "Attempt at an Explication of an Excerpt from Kant's *Critique of Judgment.*"[2] As its title implies, the primary aim of this piece was to explicate the views of the third *Critique* by paraphrasing and revising Kant's text in such a way that the difficult doctrines of that work could be liberated from Kant's obscure language and articulated in a more precise manner. It is in the introduction to the third *Critique* that Kant addresses the issue of the compatibility of theoretical and practical reason most explicitly, and, significantly, it was also this portion of the text that was of most interest to Fichte himself.[3] Since Fichte's concerns here are so closely connected to Kant's own text, we shall approach the former by first considering the main issue addressed in the latter.

The fundamental problem of the third *Critique*, as presented in the introduction, is clearly one of reconciling theoretical reason (referred to by Kant in this text as "the understanding") with practical reason (here, simply "reason"). Kant formulates the problem in terms of a potential conflict between the "legislations" (*Gesetzgebungen*) of the understanding, the source of natural concepts, and reason, the giver of the moral law. First, Kant recalls that each legislation is completely independent of the other in terms of its content. That is, the moral law does not need to seek advice from the understanding in order to tell us what we ought to do, and, conversely, the understanding provides the general laws of nature without the aid of practical reason. Second, it is clear from the results of the first *Critique* that the two faculties cannot contradict each other in what they might tell us about supersensible reality, since the understanding can make no legitimate claims to provide knowledge of things in themselves. A potential conflict does arise, however, when one considers the effects of these two legislations within the world of appearances. The principle of

---

2. GA, II.1, pp. 325–73.
3. See Fichte's letter to Weißhuhn of 1790, where he writes that he finds the introduction to be "the most obscure part of the book" and, by implication, the part most in need of reformulation (GA, III.1, pp. 188–9).

natural causality holds universally in this realm, and yet, according to Kant, practical reason also requires that its own "legislation" be realizable within the sensible world:

> There is a vast gulf fixed between the realm of the concept of nature, as the sensible, and the realm of the concept of freedom, as the supersensible. The nature of this gulf is such that it is impossible to pass from the former to the latter (by means of the theoretical use of reason) – just as if they were two different worlds, the first of which could have no influence on the second. Yet the latter *is supposed to* (*soll*) have an influence on the former. That is, the concept of freedom is supposed to realize within the sensible world the purpose proposed by its laws.[4]

Kant's point is that while the principle of natural causality is of service only within the realm of appearances, the effects of the laws of morality cannot be restricted in the same way to the noumenal world. The latter are principles that command the realization of ends, and unless morality is to be merely a relation among noumenal entities with no effects in the world we know and experience, these ends must be realizable within the phenomenal world. In order to satisfy the demands of both theoretical and practical reason, then, it must be possible to think of the sensible world as capable of exhibiting the effects of both kinds of legislation. In Kant's words, "nature must be able to be thought in such a way that the lawfulness of its form is compatible at least with the possibility of the realization within nature of purposes in accord with laws of freedom."[5] It is precisely this task to which the *Critique of Judgment* is addressed, namely, to show that it is possible and legitimate to think of the natural realm both as universally governed by the principle of natural causality *and* as embodying the effects of a rational, nonmechanistic causality. Kant goes on to elaborate the only way in which human thought can accommodate the demands of both theoretical and practical reason:

> There must be a foundation (*Grund*) for the *unity* of the supersensible that constitutes the ground of nature and that which is practically contained in the concept of freedom. The concept of this foundation, although incapable, both theoretically and practically,

---

4. Kant, *Kritik der Urteilskraft* (KU), pp. 175–6. Published in English as *Critique of Judgment*, p. 12.
5. KU, p. 176; English, p. 12.

of attaining to knowledge of it, . . . nevertheless makes possible the transition from the mode of thought in accord with the principles of one to the mode of thought in accord with the principles of the other.[6]

Of course, Kant must do more than merely *assert* the conceivability of this unity; he must convince us that there is in fact no contradiction in the view that a world governed by universal causal determination might also be one that can accommodate the effects of a completely independent set of laws, namely, those of freedom. Kant argues for the conceivability of the two kinds of legislation within one and the same world by referring to the role played by a particular kind of teleology within natural science. In the third *Critique* Kant recognizes that the legislation of the categories of the understanding, even as universally applicable in the realm of experience, is not itself sufficient to guarantee the possibility of systematic knowledge of nature according to empirical laws. The world of experience might indeed be structured according to the categories of the understanding and still be too complex – infused with too great a diversity – to be captured in terms of simple empirical laws that could then be combined into a system of natural science. The conditions for the possibility of experience laid out in the *Critique of Pure Reason* constitute a necessary but not sufficient condition for the possibility of a unified system of natural science. For the latter to be possible, the faculty of reflective judgment must supply a transcendental principle that can be derived neither from theoretical understanding nor from pure practical reason. Kant characterizes this transcendental principle in the following way:

> With respect to what is left undetermined by the general laws of nature grounded in our understanding, particular empirical laws must be regarded as if they were in accord with a unity such as they would have if an understanding (though not our own) had, for the benefit of our cognitive faculties, provided them in order to make possible a system of experience in accord with particular laws of nature.[7]

Thus, in the quest for a systematic knowledge of the empirical world, it is possible, indeed necessary, to regard the events of that world both as completely subject to natural causality and as

6. KU, p. 176; English, p. 12.   7. KU, p. 180; English, p. 16.

determined teleologically, that is, in accord with a purpose – in this case, the purpose of a hypothetical intelligence that undertook to determine the details of the empirical world in such a way that it could be known by the human mind in a system of particular empirical laws.

Kant's point with regard to natural science seems clear and, for our purposes, unobjectionable. What is not so apparent, however, is precisely how this point can be of help in the reconciliation of freedom and natural causality. In a very general sense, the example of natural science is relevant in that it shows how a kind of purposiveness (a legislation distinct from natural causality) can be attributed to the phenomena of nature without thereby violating the principle of natural causality. The crucial question, however, is whether the kind of purposiveness assumed by the idea of a systematic knowledge of nature is sufficiently analogous to the purposiveness implicit in the principles of practical reason to be able to shed any light upon the compatibility of the latter with the legislation of the understanding.

The answer to this question depends upon how one understands the particular "legislation" of practical reason that is at issue. Kant's statement of the problem, quoted above, is ambiguous in one crucial respect: In what sense are we to understand the "purposes" (*Zwecke*) that the laws of freedom command to be realized within the sensible world? It is natural to assume that the purposes referred to are simply the duties that the moral law requires rational agents to perform. On this interpretation, the task of the introduction to the *Critique of Judgment* would be to show how the commands of the moral law itself can be realized within a world that is governed by natural causality – in other words, how the phenomenal world can be rigorously determined as well as an arena in which free actions can be realized.

A second interpretation, however, takes the "purposes" proposed by the laws of freedom to refer to a particular demand made by morality that happiness in the sensible world be distributed in proportion to virtue. There is good evidence to suggest that this is the sense in which Kant understood the problem of the third *Critique*, not the least of which is that under this interpretation the purposiveness at issue becomes truly analogous to that involved in his example of natural science.[8] The presupposition that

8. Two other pieces of evidence support this interpretation of Kant's problem in the third *Critique:* (1)Under the first interpretation, the problem of the *Critique*

happiness should accord with virtue contains nothing that would necessarily violate the universality of the causal principle in nature. It merely requires an assumption to the effect that an intelligent being has predetermined the details of the natural world in such a way that the normal, causally determined course of events will also fulfill this requirement of morality.

Nevertheless, it is clear from Fichte's text that he takes Kant's problem to be the first of the two alternatives just outlined.[9] For him, the problem consists in explaining how the realization of the principles of practical reason, understood here as moral commands, can be compatible with the requirement of theoretical reason that the world of experience be universally determined. In other words, Fichte's problem becomes one of understanding how a particular subset of human actions – moral deeds – can, as events within the empirical world, be both causally determined *and* consequences of the free determination of the will.

Despite the importance of this issue, the fact remains that it is a different problem from the one Kant intended to solve in the third *Critique*. For this reason, it is easy to see why Fichte could not find satisfaction in a solution based upon the strategy of that work. Although Kant may have successfully articulated how a kind of natural teleology is compatible with the universal causal law, it is difficult to see how the kind of purposiveness involved here could help us understand what Fichte takes to be the problem at hand. The crucial difference between Kant's example of natural teleology and the realization of free, moral actions with which Fichte is concerned is that the former can be understood in

---

of Judgment collapses into the problem of the third antinomy. Not only is this unlikely – why would Kant need two distinct solutions to the same problem? – but Kant explicitly characterizes the third antinomy as directed at a different problem (KU, p. 175; English, p. 11). (2) In this and other works Kant often refers to the problem of "purposiveness in nature" and the "harmony of the laws of nature with those of freedom." In most of these passages it is clear that the problem he has in mind is that of the correspondence of happiness and virtue. For example, see Kant, *Kritik der Praktischen Vernunft* (KPV), p. 144. Published in English as *Critique of Practical Reason*, p. 150. Also, *Kritik der reinen Vernunft* (KRV), A810–11/B838–9.

9. This is made clear by statements such as the following: "The legislation of freedom is aimed only at the mere determination of the will" (GA, II.1, p. 329). Hence, Fichte takes "legislation of freedom" to refer to moral laws that present commands for the determination of the will, rather than to morality's demand that nature be determined in accord with moral purposes. See also GA, II.1, p. 347.

a way that does not require a continuous intervention of supersensible causes into the phenomenal chain of events. In the case of Fichte's problem, however, no mere principle of reflective judgment can solve what appears to be an outright contradiction between the requirements of the two forms of reason. While theoretical reason requires the effects of free decisions to be realizable within the phenomenal world, practical reason seems to rule out the possibility of an uncaused act breaking into the chain of causally governed events to initiate a new series of consequences.

Although Fichte's reading of the introduction misunderstands the specific issue that Kant intended to address in the third *Critique,* it nevertheless illuminates another important sense in which the problem of the compatibility of theoretical and practical reason arises for Critical Philosophy. This problem, however, is more closely related to the one addressed in the third antinomy in the *Critique of Pure Reason* than to the concerns of the *Critique of Judgment.* The question Kant asks in the third antinomy is whether natural causality is the only causality applicable to appearances, or whether another species of causality, freedom, might not apply as well. The dilemma Kant faces, as well as its relevance to moral philosophy, is easily understood: If morality is to have a place in the empirical world, then it must be possible to conceive of human actions within that world as free, or uncaused. Yet Kant's argument in the first half of the first *Critique* for the universal validity of the causal law in the realm of nature seems to rule out the possibility of an uncaused event within that realm. Hence, the prospects for maintaining the possibility of free events within the empirical world seem quite dim. For to hold that every empirical event is determined with strict necessity by another, temporally prior event seems to imply that the positing of freedom as a "cause" of any such event is not merely superfluous but incompatible with the necessity required by the principle of natural causality.

Although Kant attempts to resolve this difficulty by making a distinction between appearances and things in themselves, and by correlating them with natural causality and freedom, respectively, Fichte devotes a considerable portion of his early philosophical efforts to understanding how this move can solve Kant's problem. Fichte's doubts about Kant's solution center not only on the ability of the noumenal–phenomenal distinction to make intelligible the possibility of a free act occurring in the natural world; he is also concerned with the implications of applying such a distinction to the practical subject itself: Does the radical distinction between appearances and things in themselves leave room for any kind of connection between the noumenal and empirical selves which could make moral action a coherent possibility?[10] Although worries about the compatibility of Kant's accounts of theoretical and practical reason constituted an important motivating factor for the young Fichte, as well as for many of his contemporaries, this sense of the unity of reason is not the most important for understanding the philosophical system that he ultimately develops. Rather, the systems that Fichte attempted to construct from 1793 on are concerned primarily with the unity of reason in two different senses (the second and third theses outlined earlier), each of which asserts a deeper unity than mere *compatibility*. Nevertheless, the problems underlying Fichte's early misgivings about Kant's two accounts of reason do not simply drop out of view in his later thought. Although the issue does not reappear in Fichte's systematic works in precisely the form considered here, the same basic question – can Critical Philosophy provide an adequate defense of morality and human freedom? – occupies a central place in later texts as well. For, as we shall eventually see, in one form or another it is this issue that motivates the project of unifying theoretical and practical reason in each of the different guises that that project takes on.

10. The first of these concerns is found in both versions of Fichte's first major work, *Attempt at a Critique of All Revelation* (1792). Original at GA, I.1, pp.15–161; and SW, V, pp. 9–172. See especially pp. 118–22 (GA, I.1, pp. 69–74; SW, V, pp. 106–12), where, in the context of considering the notion of revelation, Fichte attempts to make sense of the possibility of the effects of a supernatural cause appearing within the empirical world: "Is it even conceivable that something *outside* of nature can have a causality *within* nature? We shall answer this question, in part, in order to shed a bit more light upon the still obscure doctrine of the possibility of the coexistence of necessity in accord with natural laws and freedom in accord with moral laws" (p. 118; GA, I.1, p. 69; SW, V, pp. 106–7). The latter issue is Fichte's main concern in the Creuzer review of 1793, where Fichte eventually concludes that the only way available to Kant of understanding the relation between noumenal and phenomenal subjects is in terms of "a pre-established harmony between the determinations of freedom and those of the law of nature," the foundation *(Grund)* of which lies neither in nature nor in freedom, "but only in a higher law which subsumes and unites both under itself" (SW, VIII, p. 415). It is, of course, impossible to attain any insight into how this higher law can bring the elements of two completely independent realms into a relationship of correspondence, but theoretical reason is impotent to prove the impossibility of such a law, and, in the absence of any other possibility of relating the subject as noumenon to its existence as an appearance, practical reason requires such a belief.

The systematic unity of reason

In the second of the three theses outlined earlier, theoretical and practical reason are understood to constitute a unity if the principles of each can be derived within a single system of philosophy, all parts of which are deducible from a chain of arguments arising out of one first principle. It is this conception of the unity of reason that figures most prominently in Fichte's earliest efforts at constructing a philosophical system. Thus, Fichte's attempt to demonstrate the unity of reason takes the form of a search for a first principle capable of founding a system of philosophy that encompasses both theoretical and practical reason. While it is clear that such a project is distinct from one that merely aims to prove the compatibility of the two forms of reason, it is not so clear why demonstrating the unity of reason in this sense should be regarded as an important, or even desirable, goal for philosophy. What precisely is to be gained by bringing together theoretical and practical reason within a single system of philosophy? In order to answer this question we must briefly consider the historical context in which Fichte's idea for such a project originated.

Fichte's quest for a single principle of reason has its immediate roots in the thought of K. L. Reinhold, who by the early 1790s had become, apart from Kant himself, the most influential expositor and proponent of Critical Philosophy.[11] During this period Reinhold's principal philosophical goal was to unify the disparate elements of Kant's thought into a more systematic philosophy, and central to this effort was the search for a first principle from which all of philosophy could be derived. Reinhold's actual attempts at systematizing philosophy focused primarily on Kant's first *Critique*, and especially on the task of tracing the two sources of theoretical knowledge – the forms of sensible intuition and the categories of the understanding – back to a single common root. Yet there is no reason why this same strategy could not be followed to demonstrate a fundamental affinity between the two faculties of reason as well. If it were possible to discover a single principle capable of grounding *all* of philosophy, then theoretical and practical reason would be "unified" in the sense that each could be shown to derive from a common first principle. In the following chapter we shall examine in greater detail Fichte's initial attempts

11. Most significant here is Reinhold (1789).

to realize this general conception of a philosophical system.[12] For now it is more important to understand why Reinhold and Fichte considered this kind of systematicity to be an important goal of philosophy.

The idea that there might exist a fundamental principle shared by both theoretical and practical reason does not originate with Fichte, or even with Reinhold, but is suggested already by Kant in the *Critique of Practical Reason*. In a notoriously obscure passage toward the middle of that work Kant states that comparisons of the respective structures of the first two critiques "legitimately arouse the expectation that perhaps one day it will be possible to arrive at insight into the unity of the whole faculty of pure reason (theoretical as well as practical) and to derive everything from one principle."[13] In the second *Critique,* however, Kant does not go on to consider in any more detail how the two faculties of reason might be shown to proceed from a common ground. In fact, apart from this vague allusion to the possible unity of reason, Kant never takes up this question in precisely the same form again. Why, then, does Fichte regard the discovery of a single principle of reason as an unfinished and necessary task for Critical Philosophy? In other words, why is it that what for Kant was mere conjecture was to become for Fichte a statement of one of philosophy's necessary and most urgent tasks?

The reason given by Kant for his suggestion that searching for a common principle of reason would be an appropriate philosophical goal is that such a search springs from "the unavoidable need of human reason, which only finds complete satisfaction in a perfectly systematic unity of its knowledge."[14] Since it is the task of reason to unify particulars by subsuming them under principles of ever greater generality, philosophy can be completely satisfied with itself only when it has succeeded in recognizing the essential commonalities among what initially appear to be wholly disparate entities. At the same time, however, it must be emphasized that for Kant the fact that reason is compelled to search for systematic unity does not guarantee that such unity can actually be found. Reason's need for unity is sufficient to legitimize Fichte's

---

12. As we shall see in Chapter 2, Fichte's initial idea was to attempt to deduce the principles of both theoretical and practical reason as necessary conditions of the unity of consciousness. Hence, on this view, the unity of consciousness would serve as the first principle of all of philosophy.

13. KPV, p. 91; English, p. 94.   14. KPV, p. 91; English, p. 94.

quest for a single principle of reason as an enterprise that is *consistent* with the spirit of Critical Philosophy, but it does not imply that Kant's inability to find such a common ground necessarily constitutes a defect in his system. The absence of a single principle for the whole of philosophy may be regarded as a disappointment but not, strictly speaking, as a failure.

For Fichte, however, the demand for a single principle of reason acquires an urgency that seems inappropriate for a goal that, from Kant's perspective, remained nothing more than a regulative ideal. It is understandable that philosophy would rejoice at such a discovery if it were made, but it is unclear why it should become one of the main preoccupations of post-Kantian philosophy. I shall argue that the task of finding a first principle capable of grounding both theoretical and practical reason takes on such significance for Fichte because he comes to believe that the discovery of such a principle will enable him to provide a more solid defense of Kant's moral theory than Kant himself was able to give. This view derives from Reinhold's general notion of a philosophical system and especially from his belief that uniting disparate elements into a single system would allow one to discern important relations between those elements that would otherwise remain hidden. Thus, in the field of theoretical reason Reinhold hoped that a truly systematic version of Critical Philosophy would yield not only definitive proofs of the validity of each individual category of the understanding but also a demonstration of the completeness of Kant's set of categories. Applied to the case at hand, a system that could comprehend all of philosophy as proceeding from a single principle might also be able to settle issues concerning the relationship between theoretical and practical reason that Kant's version of Critical Philosophy is unable to resolve. More specifically, Fichte's hope seems to be that if the principles of practical reason could be shown to occupy a particular place within a unitary and rigorously deduced philosophical system, then those principles would acquire a kind of grounding that they do not possess in isolation from the system. In other words, to locate the tenets of practical reason within such a system might also enable Fichte to prove their validity. As we shall see in greater detail in the following chapter, Fichte's first attempt (in the Gebhard review) to find a common principle for all of reason reveals very clearly how, at least for the young Fichte, the task of defending Kant's view of morality converges with that of deriving all of philosophy from one principle. For now our task is to understand the sense in which Fichte believed Kant's practical philosophy to be in need of a more stable foundation.

Fichte's criticism of the foundations of Kant's moral theory is articulated for the first time in the Gebhard review of 1793.[15] In this piece Fichte turns his attention to what he believes to be a crucial problem of Kant's philosophy, one that calls into question "nothing less than the general validity of the Kantian moral principle."[16] The unresolved difficulty to which Fichte refers is the absence within Kant's moral philosophy of a positive proof of the practical nature of pure reason. At the end of the Gebhard review Fichte explicitly formulates what for him is the central task yet to be accomplished by Critical Philosophy: "It must be proved *that* reason is practical."[17] This assertion raises two questions in need of closer attention: First, what must be shown about pure reason in order to prove that it is practical? And second, why are Kant's own arguments for this claim insufficient?

The first question can be made more precise if reformulated as follows: Is the human agent capable of being motivated to act by some incentive other than those that are merely sensuous and hence supplied to her from an external source (nature) in accord with natural causal laws? That is, can certain human actions be determined by a purely rational incentive derived from the awareness of a law of pure reason that the human agent, as a rational being, legislates for herself? It is clear that both Kant and Fichte want to answer these questions in the affirmative, for they agree that a positive answer to each is necessary in order to sustain two closely related beliefs, namely, that human beings have moral obligations and that they are capable of genuine autonomy. Before considering these connections in closer detail, let us turn to the second issue raised earlier concerning the inadequacy of Kant's own arguments in support of his claim that pure reason has a practical capacity.

---

15. GA, I.2, pp. 21–9; SW, VIII, pp. 418–26. This work is a review of F. H. Gebhard's book *Ueber die sittliche Güte aus uninteressiertem Wohlwollen* (1792).
16. SW, VIII, p. 418.
17. SW, VIII, p. 425. Fichte consistently uses the term 'practical reason' to refer to what Kant called 'pure practical reason' and contrasted to 'empirical practical reason'. I shall follow Fichte's usage here, so that 'practical reason' should be taken to signify practical reason in its pure (i.e., empirically unconditioned) form.

Fichte's main objection to Kant's position is that the mere presence within consciousness of a moral feeling is itself insufficient to establish that pure reason is practical. In other words, Fichte's claim in the Gebhard review is that a proof of the practical nature of pure reason cannot be attained simply by appealing to facts of consciousness. An awareness of the moral "ought" is not by itself sufficient to demonstrate that pure reason has a practical capacity, for the mere presence of "the moral feeling" (*das sittliche Gefühl*)[18] implies nothing about its origin – that is, the feeling of moral necessity may indeed be present within consciousness, but it does not at the same time proclaim itself as the product of pure reason. Thus, both Kant and his opponents could conceivably agree upon the facts of moral consciousness and still disagree over whether those facts point to the existence of a faculty of practical reason. For example, the moral feeling might just as well be explained as a manifestation of a "fundamental drive of the mind" (*ein Grundtrieb des Gemüts*) or, in other words, as the product of a natural drive that, like the drive for pleasure, is simply a component of human nature.[19] If explained in this way, moral feeling could still be perceived as qualitatively distinct from other kinds of feelings such as pleasure and pain, but it would nevertheless share one crucial characteristic with these more obviously sensuous feelings: As the products of natural drives, both would have to be regarded as simply given to the subject. Thus, for Fichte the feeling of moral necessity *is* a fact of consciousness, but that this feeling derives from a faculty of pure reason is not itself revealed by consciousness and, indeed, represents only one possible interpretation of it.

The philosophical import of this challenge becomes clearer when one sees that, for Fichte, the crucial distinction between attributing moral feeling to a faculty of practical reason and regarding it as an effect of a natural drive is that the former view implies that moral consciousness derives from "an absolute self-activity of the human spirit," while the latter implies that the feeling is given to a passive subject from without.[20] Thus, on the first

---

18. Fichte also uses the expression "the feeling of moral necessity (the *ought*)" and "the feeling of the absolute right" (*jenes Gefühl des schlechthin Rechtes*) (SW, VIII, pp. 423–4).
19. SW, VIII, p. 420.   20. SW, VIII, p. 420.

account, an action for which the moral feeling served as the determining incentive could be considered autonomous in the sense
that the subject's will would have been determined by a self-given
incentive; on the second account, where moral feeling is simply
the result of natural drives, a deed motivated by moral feeling
would be no more "self-determined" than those acts motivated by
other, more obviously natural incentives. At issue in this debate,
then, is nothing less than the nature of human freedom and the
question as to whether the human being is capable of genuine
self-determination: Is freedom to be understood as limited to the
ability to choose among given incentives, or is the human being
capable of supplying himself with his own practical ends? Viewed
in this light, the gravity of Fichte's challenge becomes apparent,
for in the absence of a proof that the moral feeling within us
derives from practical reason, Critical Philosophy cannot conclusively establish the real possibility of human autonomy. Thus, the
question of the existence of practical reason is bound up with the
validity of the moral law itself. For if the human being were incapable of acting on the basis of reason alone and therefore had no
capacity for genuine autonomy, then "real morality would be
destroyed," and the belief that we have moral obligations would
be a "demonstrable illusion."[21]

It is clear that Fichte's criticism of Kant here is directed primarily at the version of his position laid out in the *Critique of Practical
Reason*. To demonstrate that pure reason has a practical capacity
Kant appeals there not to a "moral feeling," as Fichte would have
it, but to an undeniable "fact of reason." Kant describes this fact
of reason as the consciousness of the fundamental law of morality
and as "the only fact of pure reason," which "thereby proclaims
itself as an original giver of laws" (*als ursprünglich gesetzgebend*). In
another passage Kant characterizes this fact of reason as a principle that "forces itself upon us as a synthetic a priori principle
which rests upon no intuition, either pure or empirical."[22] Starting from this original, "undeniable" fact Kant argues that a moral
command cannot be valid for the human being unless one assumes
that pure reason, apart from all natural inclination, is capable of
determining the will. In other words, the immediate and undeniable consciousness of moral obligation to which Kant appeals in

---

21. SW, VIII, p. 424.   22. KPV, p. 31; English, p. 31.

the second *Critique* is held to establish the reality of practical reason, since in the absence of such a faculty, moral action, and therefore moral obligation as well, would not be possible.

On the latter point – that morality requires a faculty of practical reason – Fichte is in complete agreement with Kant. What he objects to is that the argument for practical reason rests merely upon an appeal to a fact of consciousness. Although Fichte grants the reality of the moral feeling as a fact of consciousness, his objection is that it cannot carry the weight that Kant wants it to. Perhaps Fichte's point can best be put in the following way: An analysis of what we mean by the "ought" and of how we understand moral obligation does indeed show that if we regard ourselves as subject to moral obligations, we are also required to believe in practical reason and therefore in the possibility of autonomy as well. The question left unanswered by this analysis, however, is whether the belief that we are bound by moral obligations might not itself be an illusion.

Fichte's rejection of Kant's appeal to the notion of a "fact of reason" is most plausibly understood as based upon the belief that, in taking this position, Kant fails to carry out a thoroughgoing, consistent application of his own Critical principles to the field of moral philosophy. That is, Kant's treatment of reason in the second *Critique* seems to stand in conflict with his procedure in the first. For the former characterizes the moral law as a synthetic principle, yet Kant does not ground this synthetic proposition in either of the two ways available to the Critical Philosopher of the first *Critique* – namely, by pointing to an intuition upon which it rests or by providing a transcendental deduction.[23] Furthermore, in the "Transcendental Dialectic" of the *Critique of Pure Reason* Kant asserts the need for a critical examination of the beliefs to which theoretical reason inevitably leads us. This he does by asking whether, despite the necessity with which reason arrives at these beliefs, they might nevertheless be illusory. On what grounds does our belief in the validity of the moral law elude this same critical examination and escape the demand for a deduction? What

23. See also Kant, *Grundlegung zur Metaphysik der Sitten* (GMS), 420. Published in English as *Groundwork of the Metaphysic of Morals*, pp. 87–8. Significantly, though, Kant speaks here of demonstrating only the *possibility* of a practical a priori synthetic proposition, not of proving that there is one (i.e., that we do in fact have moral obligations), as Fichte seems to have in mind.

the young Fichte seeks, then, is a stronger defense of the validity of our belief in the reality of moral obligation or, in other words, a more rigorous deduction of the moral law than is provided by Kant in the second *Critique*.

Although the position implicit in Kant's doctrine of a "fact of reason" denies that such a proof is necessary, it is important to note that Kant espoused this view only after a futile, decade-long search for precisely the kind of deduction demanded by Fichte.[24] But the position at which Kant eventually arrived – that the validity and binding force of the moral law require no external justification – failed to satisfy the young Fichte, and the quest for a more substantial proof of practical reason came to be one of the most powerful motivating forces behind the development of his own philosophical system, one expression of which, as we shall see more clearly in Chapter 2, consists in the attempt to show that both theoretical and practical reason rest upon a single first principle. Although the hope behind this search for a more rigorous deduction of the moral law may not accord with Kant's position in the *Critique of Practical Reason*, it is at least consistent with the spirit of Critical Philosophy in general. Furthermore, in the absence of a definitive argument on Kant's part that such a proof is in principle unattainable, there is nothing to prevent one from assuming that, although Kant himself was unable to discover it, a more conclusive proof of practical reason might lie within philosophy's grasp.

Fichte's preoccupation with the unity of reason in the sense just described differs from the first version of his project in the following crucial respect: In attempting to demonstrate the compatibility of theoretical and practical reason Fichte is concerned with proving the *possibility* of practical reason – of explaining how, given the determinism implied by theoretical reason, it is possible also to believe that human beings are free in the sense of being capable of moral autonomy. The motivation behind Fichte's quest to demonstrate the systematic unity of reason aims at something stronger, namely, a positive proof of the *reality* of practical reason. Formulated in this way, however, it becomes clear that the difference between these two projects is overshadowed by what

---

24. That such a project was a major concern of Kant's between 1770 and 1785 is demonstrated by a number of such attempts in the *Reflexionen* as well as by traces of this project still to be found in Section III of the *Groundwork*. For a thorough account of these attempts see Henrich (1960, pp. 77–115).

they have in common. For both are ultimately motivated by one basic concern: the desire to uphold Kant's conception of autonomy against those who deny that the belief in human freedom can be rationally defended.

The structural identity of theoretical and practical reason

In the remainder of this chapter we shall consider, although only briefly, the third sense in which the theme of the unity of reason appears in Fichte's thought. Although I shall argue that it is ultimately this third conception which is most important for understanding Fichte's theory of subjectivity, it has no significant presence in his earliest writings. For this reason we shall restrict ourselves to a brief sketch of this notion of unity and postpone filling in the details until the end of Chapter 2, after we have traced the particular developments of Fichte's philosophical system.

To uphold the "unity of reason" in this third sense is to claim that theoretical and practical reason are not two distinct faculties but rather two forms, or "employments," of a single faculty of reason. There is a sense, then, in which this notion of unity implies the existence of a deeper affinity between theoretical and practical reason than what is envisioned in the previous two conceptions. In the first place, the relation asserted here is clearly stronger than mere compatibility. Moreover, it involves more than the claim that the principles of theoretical and practical reason can be derived from one first principle, or even that both can be brought together within a single philosophical system. What is asserted here is that each faculty has in some sense the same internal structure. The relation between theoretical and practical reason on this view is one of genuine *unity,* implying a fundamental *identity* between them. The notion of a deep, structural unity between two apparently disparate subjective faculties finds expression in Kant's well-known remark in the introduction to the first *Critique* that "the two stems of human knowledge, namely, *sensibility* and *understanding,* perhaps spring from a common, but to us unknown, root."[25] Although what Kant alludes to here is a unity

25. KRV, A15/B29. See also KRV, A649–50/B677–8, where Kant makes a similar suggestion with regard to the diverse faculties of imagination, pleasure, desire, etc.

within theoretical reason itself, there is no obvious reason why the same idea might not also be applicable to the relationship between theoretical and practical reason. In fact, in at least one place in his published writings Kant explicitly endorses the thesis of the unity of reason in precisely the sense we are currently examining:

> ... a critique of pure practical reason, if it is to be complete, requires, on my view, that we should be able at the same time to show the unity of practical and theoretical reason in a common principle, since in the end there can only be one and the same reason, which is to be differentiated solely in its application.[26]

Kant's insistence that "there can only be one reason, which is . . . differentiated solely in its application" can be considered the classical formulation of this third sense of the unity of reason; and, as I shall argue later, it is this provocative but unelaborated idea of Kant's that Fichte attempts to work out. Such a project, then, would take as its most basic question the following: Is it possible to comprehend theoretical and practical reason as two forms of a single faculty of reason? Or, alternatively, does a single structure – a structure of reason in general – underlie both the theoretical and practical uses of reason?

Of course, it is by no means obvious from this brief characterization what precisely it would mean to attribute to theoretical and practical reason an identical "structure." One way in which a Kantian might attempt to fill in the details of such a claim is by arguing that reason has an identical function in both its theoretical and practical employments, since in both cases it bestows a kind of unity upon some given manifold content – in the first case, a manifold of intuitions, in the second, a manifold of natural desires. Although this is not the particular direction taken by Fichte, it nevertheless qualifies as an example of the unity that can be attributed to reason in the sense under consideration here. In the view that Fichte will ultimately develop, the identical structure of reason will be articulated in his most distinctive philosophical notion, that of the self-positing subject. As we shall see in Chapter 2, Fichte comes to believe that his theory of subjectivity can demonstrate the essential unity of reason by showing that the subject's theoretical and practical faculties are derivative of the same fundamental activity of the mind, which he calls "self-positing."

26. GMS, p. 391; English, p. 59.

This way of unifying theoretical and practical reason can easily be seen as a continuation of the philosophical project (undertaken by Leibniz, continued by Wolff, and alluded to by Kant in the earlier quote) of showing that all of the subject's capacities derive from a single fundamental power (*Grundkraft*) of the soul.[27] Although Kant in the *Critique of Pure Reason* denies that the unity of the subjective capacities can be guaranteed in advance of any actual philosophical inquiry, he does admit the legitimacy of philosophy's endeavor to demonstrate this kind of unity among the various faculties, and this for a reason similar to one mentioned earlier, namely, that the "principle of reason calls upon us to bring about such unity as completely as possible."[28] Thus, the unity of reason in this third sense is taken by Kant to constitute a kind of regulative ideal that philosophy by its very nature must strive to attain (even though, of course, it may not actually be able to realize it). Viewed in this context, Fichte's attempt to demonstrate the unity of reason in this deepest sense can be seen not only as a continuation of a project central to the tradition of modern philosophy, but, at least in its basic intent, as one that is consistent with the spirit of Critical Philosophy as well. The question remains, however, whether this particular version of Fichte's philosophical task also responds in some way to his concerns about philosophy's ability to defend human freedom. We shall return to this question at the end of the following chapter, after we have examined in greater detail how the specific features of his undertaking emerge out of his attempts to find a proof of practical reason and to ground all of philosophy in a single first principle.

27. See Henrich (1955, pp. 28–69).
28. KRV, A649/B677. In the first version of the introduction to the *Critique of Judgment* Kant also characterizes such an attempt as one which "is undertaken in a genuinely philosophical spirit" (p. 206).

—⇥ ⇤—

2

THE DEVELOPMENT OF
FICHTE'S PROJECT
FROM 1793 TO 1799

The purpose of this chapter is to trace the development that Fichte's philosophical project undergoes during the period from 1793 to 1799. Our ultimate goal will be to understand how his conception of that project as a theory of subjectivity emerges out of earlier attempts to uphold the thesis of the unity of theoretical and practical reason. As we shall see, in his early philosophical writings Fichte concentrates primarily on the task of demonstrating the unity of reason in the second of the three senses outlined in Chapter 1 (where both theoretical and practical reason are to be brought together into one system that proceeds from a single first principle). By 1797, however, Fichte comes to have a different understanding of his enterprise, one that embodies the third sense of the unity of reason, according to which theoretical and practical reason are to be comprehended as a single faculty, each of which exhibits the same "structure" of reason in general. The story of this transformation is significantly complicated by the fact that for Fichte the issue of the unity of reason is inextricably bound up with his wish to find a positive proof of the reality of practical reason. Initially, it is the latter concern that dominates his attempts to construct a new philosophical system. In order to understand how Fichte intends to carry out the tasks he sets for himself, it will be necessary to investigate the general structure and method of his most significant philosophical achievement, the Doctrine of Science, or, as I shall refer to it here, the *Wissenschafts-lehre*.[1] Our examination of Fichte's system will lead us to focus primarily upon his notion of a first principle of philosophy. Specifically, we shall attempt to answer the following questions: What precisely is meant to be asserted by Fichte's first principle? On what grounds is that starting point justified? What relation is there between the first principle and the other truths "deduced" within that system?

Unfortunately, there exists very little consensus among interpreters of Fichte as to how even these most fundamental questions are to be answered.[2] My own approach to understanding the *Wissenschaftslehre* is based upon the conviction that much of this disagreement can be resolved by viewing the texts of the period from 1793 to 1799 not as representatives of a single, coherent system, but rather as stages in a tumultuous process of insight, self-criticism, and revision, all of which are aimed at the development of a more consistent philosophical position. In other words, it is my view that the widespread controversy over the general nature of the *Wissenschaftslehre* stems in part from the often unacknowledged fact that Fichte's own conception of his project underwent a number of radical changes. The notion of a fundamental development in Fichte's position is already universally accepted, insofar as commentators generally distinguish between Fichte's views prior to 1800 and the system developed immediately after the Atheism Controversy.[3] What is less widely recognized, however, is that the general conception of the *Wissenschaftslehre* was in a state of continual evolution even before 1800, especially in the first five years of its existence. Not only are there developments in the system's *method* (i.e., in its starting point and strategy of

---

1. I shall use the term *Wissenschaftslehre* to refer to Fichte's system in the abstract, as opposed to specific texts that expound the doctrines of that system. The latter will be referred to by full titles or, in the case of the first published version, by the abbreviation WL 1794.

2. For a good discussion of the different (German) schools of interpretation see Baumanns (1972, pp. 15–47). Missing from this account, however, is a discussion of the main French current of Fichte interpretation, represented by Alexis Philonenko, Luc Ferry, and Alain Renaut.

3. Of course, even here there is disagreement over whether the post-1800 versions of the *Wissenschaftslehre* constitute a discontinuous rupture with the earlier period or whether they are to be seen merely as further developments of what remains essentially a single project.

argumentation), but its very *aims* (or at least the priority accorded to its various goals), undergo considerable revision as well. Since our concern in this study is to examine Fichte's most advanced position prior to the break of 1800, it will be necessary both to distinguish the different stages of Fichte's early development and to understand the reasons behind these changes. Retracing Fichte's development will constitute the largest part of the present chapter. The point, however, is not merely to narrate the history of Fichte's early years, but to enable us to reconstruct the general outline of what I am claiming to be the most interesting aspect of Fichte's project, his attempt to construct a "theory of subjectivity."

For the purposes of our discussion Fichte's development before 1800 will be divided into three major phases: (1) the presystematic writings prior to 1794; (2) the *Wissenschaftslehre* of 1794; and (3) the system of 1797–9. The first period extends from the beginning of Fichte's philosophical career to the point just before the publication of the first of his systematic writings. The texts of greatest interest here are the collections of unpublished notes entitled "Eigene Meditationen über Elementar-Philosophie" and "Praktische Philosophie" (1793–4), as well as the Gebhard review of 1793.[4] The second period is represented primarily by the first published version of Fichte's system, *Foundation of the Entire Wissenschaftslehre (Grundlage der gesammten Wissenschaftslehre,* 1794–5), but includes as well two minor texts that are directly associated with that system, the *Aenesidemus* review (1794) and *Concerning the Concept of the Wissenschaftslehre (Ueber den Begriff der Wissenschaftslehre,* 1794).[5] The final and, for our interpretation, most important stage is more difficult to demarcate precisely, because it is composed of a number of lesser known works, both published and unpublished. The published works include the two introductions to the *Wissenschaftslehre* (both from 1797) and "Attempt at a New Presentation of the *Wissenschaftslehre*" (1797).[6] The principal unpublished sources are two distinct sets of students' notes taken during

4. "Eigene Meditationen" and "Praktische Philosophie" are published in GA, II.3, pp. 21–266. The Gebhard review is discussed in Chapter 1.
5. All three texts are found both in SW, I, pp. 1–328, and in GA, I.2, pp. 41–67, 106–461. The *Grundlage* appears in English as *The Science of Knowledge.* The latter two are translated by Daniel Breazeale in *Fichte: Early Philosophical Writings,* pp. 59–77; 94–135.
6. SW, I, pp. 417–534. English translations of the two introductions appear in *The Science of Knowledge.* In distinguishing between the system of 1794 and a second system of 1797–9, I am essentially following the suggestion of Perrinjaquet

Fichte's academic lectures in 1796–9 on what he considered to be the second formulation of his system, the *Wissenschaftslehre nova methodo*.[7] Another published work, *System of the Doctrine of Morals* (1798), will not be discussed here, but in later chapters will be considered as part of the system of this third period.

The presystematic period

As mentioned earlier, the search for a proof of the practical nature of reason is the dominating concern of Fichte's presystematic writings. During this phase Fichte also asserts the unity of reason, in the second sense distinguished in Chapter 1, insofar as he attempts to show that the unity of consciousness can function as the "first principle" of both theoretical and practical reason. As we shall see, however, this quest for a single principle of reason is important to Fichte primarily because he believes that the discovery of such a principle holds the key to a proof of practical reason. In Chapter 1 we examined Fichte's early criticism of Kant's inability to prove the reality of practical reason. What is of interest to us now is the way that Fichte envisioned solving this problem in the period before the development of the *Wissenschaftslehre*. To this end we must turn again to the Gebhard review, which, in addition to setting forth Fichte's critique of Kant's position, contains a preliminary sketch of how the young Fichte thought such a proof could be carried out.

Fichte's proposal for a proof of practical reason consists of four brief lines:

> The human being (*der Mensch*) is given to consciousness as a unity (as an I); this fact can be explained only by presupposing an absolutely unconditioned in him; therefore one must assume the

(1985, pp. 7–18). It has been conclusively demonstrated by Perrinjaquet and others that the two introductions of 1797 belong to the later system with respect to both chronology and content. Although an attentive reading of these introductions provides ample reason to distinguish the conception of the *Wissenschaftslehre* presented therein from that carried out in 1794, this difference has been obscured for English speakers by the unfortunate decision of the translators of the *Grundlage der gesammten Wissenschaftslehre* to place the 1797 introductions before the text of 1794, as if the former constituted an introduction to the system expounded in 1794.

7. *Wissenschaftslehre nova methodo: Kollegnachschrift K. Chr. Fr. Krause 1798/99*. The second set of notes appears in GA, IV.2, pp. 1–267.

existence of an absolutely unconditioned in the human being. But such an absolutely unconditioned is a [faculty of] practical reason.[8]

The argument advanced here is far from compelling. Fichte himself tacitly acknowledges the inadequacy of his demonstration by prefacing it with the following qualifier: "Such a proof [that is, of practical reason] would have to go something like this." In other words, Fichte's suggestion should be regarded as a sketch of a philosophical program that has yet to be carried out rather than as a realization of that project. For this reason we shall set aside for now the question of the validity of Fichte's argument and focus instead upon the structure and aims of such a proof.

Let us begin by noting the general structure of the proposed argument. First, the proof begins with a "fact" (*Tatsache*) and, more specifically, with a fact that is "given to consciousness." From there it proceeds to deduce the reality of something (practical reason) that, according to the argument, must be assumed in order to explain the possibility of that fact. Thus, the proof Fichte proposes here is intended as a transcendental argument similar to Kant's mode of argumentation in the *Critique of Pure Reason*. It begins with a fact of consciousness that presumably will be universally admitted and argues toward its conclusion by elaborating the conditions that make that fact possible. A second feature of the proof to be noted is the nature of the fact that serves as its starting point. Here the terseness of Fichte's sketch gives rise to some degree of ambiguity, for it is not immediately clear in what sense Fichte understands the "unity" of the human being that constitutes the initial fact. Nevertheless, for reasons that will become clearer below,[9] the most plausible way of understanding Fichte's aim here is to take this "unity" to refer to the formal unity of consciousness associated with Kant's doctrine of transcendental apperception. In other words, the unity singled out by Fichte in this early phase is nothing more than the unity that a subject's diverse representations possess by belonging to a single consciousness.[10]

8. SW, VIII, p. 425.
9. The most important of these reasons is that in his "Eigene Meditationen" Fichte explicitly takes the "unity" at issue to be the unity of apperception.
10. It is worth pointing out here that Fichte obviously understands this unity as a *fact* "given to consciousness" as well as a transcendental condition for the possibility of experience in general.

Finally, let us consider the goals that Fichte's argument aims to achieve. It is not difficult to understand the sense in which such an argument, if successful, would constitute a proof of practical reason, since it attempts to show that practical reason is a necessary condition for the possibility of the formal unity of experience in general. Less obvious, but surely of great importance to Fichte as well, is the fact that such an argument would constitute a significant step toward achieving his goal of unifying theoretical and practical reason into a single, comprehensive system of philosophy. This intention is expressed in Fichte's remark that "such a proof . . . could easily be the foundation of *all* philosophical knowledge."[11] Unfortunately, in the Gebhard review itself Fichte says nothing more specific about how a proof of practical reason could be construed as a foundation for the whole of philosophy. My suggestion (which, as we shall see, is borne out in his initial position in the "Eigene Meditationen") is that Fichte envisions a philosophical system in which the principles of both practical and theoretical reason could be deduced as transcendental conditions of a single "fact," the unity of consciousness.[12] In this case the "unification of theoretical and practical reason" would take on a quite specific meaning, one that is already familiar to us from Chapter 1: The two faculties of reason would be unified in the sense that the principles of each could be deduced (transcendentally) within a system that begins from a single starting point, which would thus constitute the first principle of all of philosophy. Hence, Fichte's rather vague suggestions in the Gebhard review reveal the outline of a systematic program in which the tasks of proving practical reason and demonstrating the unity of reason (in at least one of its senses) converge in a single project. For if it could be shown that both theoretical and practical reason were necessary conditions for the unity of consciousness, then Fichte could claim to have satisfied reason's demand for unity among its principles while at the same time rectifying one of the most troubling deficiencies in Kant's system – the lack of a proof of practical reason.

Although one might be tempted to dismiss Fichte's schematic remarks in the Gebhard review as "presystematic" and therefore

11. SW, VIII, p. 425.
12. Here the unity of consciousness is (implicitly) regarded by Fichte as the first principle of theoretical reason in the sense that the validity of the categories within objective experience can be established by showing that the application of the categories is a necessary condition for a unified consciousness.

largely irrelevant to his more mature positions, there is clear evidence that the ideas expressed in this early article also informed Fichte's initial attempts to construct the system that was to evolve into the *Wissenschaftslehre* of 1794. This evidence is found in Fichte's "Eigene Meditationen über Elementar-Philosophie," a loosely connected and extremely circuitous set of unpublished notes in which Fichte attempts to clarify to himself how Reinhold's project of founding and constructing an *Elementar-Philosophie*, a complete and unitary system of transcendental idealism, could be realized. Fichte begins his search for a truly systematic philosophy by defining the notion of an *Elementar-Philosophie* in the following way:

> There might be *certain fundamental rules, universal rules,* which apply to *everything that occurs in the mind* – For: everything must be assimilated *(aufgenommen)* to the subjective unity; it occurs in a single mind; therefore everything must be assimilable to this subjective unity and everything must be in agreement at least *with this unity and with the conditions of this unity* (if such conditions can be found). These conditions, if they can be known, constitute an *Elementar-Philosophie.*[13]

Both the starting point and the goal of the projected system are clearly stated in Fichte's question to himself:

> Can one prove the categories and the forms of sensibility, time and space, as Reinhold wanted – sensibility, understanding, reason, the faculty of knowledge, the faculty of desire – can the necessity of all these things be demonstrated? Or, more specifically, can the whole of philosophy be constructed upon a single fact? . . . Is it possible to think of a path [which proceeds] from the unity of apperception up to the practical legislation of reason?[14]

These passages clearly reveal that Fichte originally conceived of his system as a single chain of arguments that would begin from "subjective unity" – or, what is the same here, "the unity of apperception" – and terminate with a deduction of the faculty of practical reason. Furthermore, the elements that comprise this system ("everything that occurs in the mind") are to be deduced by showing that each (including practical reason) constitutes one of the necessary conditions for the possibility of the unity of consciousness.

13. GA, II.3, p. 21.   14. GA, II.3, p. 26.

What remains unclear is how these deductions, especially in the case of practical reason, are to be accomplished. If we recall Fichte's remarks in the Gebhard review, it seems likely that the basic thought behind his intended proof is something like the following: The unity among a subject's representations that is inherent in consciousness cannot be understood as a feature of experience that is passively received by the subject from without, but must be regarded instead as a product of the subject's own spontaneity. Insofar as subjective activity constitutes the conditions under which experience alone is possible, it necessarily stands outside of that experience and is therefore empirically unconditioned. Although Fichte does not argue for this claim, there is nothing in it that is not already contained within the doctrines of Kant's first *Critique*. The puzzling point, and the crucial one as well, is what appears to be Fichte's illegitimate leap from the spontaneity of the theoretical subject to the conclusion that this unconditioned activity is identical to a faculty of practical reason. There is no apparent reason to assume that the kind of spontaneity invoked by Kant in his account of theoretical reason – that is, a spontaneity that unifies diverse representations into a single consciousness – is also *practical* in the sense required by Kant's account of morality, namely, as producing an incentive for action that is capable of determining the will independently of sensibility.

Although Fichte is not much clearer in the "Eigene Meditationen" as to how the link between the unity of apperception and the moral law of practical reason is to be made, his frequent references to the categorical imperative as the "highest unity" of consciousness[15] suggest that some such connection might be drawn by pointing out the similar roles theoretical and practical reason play as "unifiers" of the manifold of experience. Although Fichte was surely unaware of it, this same connection had already suggested itself to Kant, who devoted considerable energy in his *Reflexionen* to finding a transcendental deduction of the categorical imperative from the starting point of pure apperception.[16] The analogy between theoretical and practical reason that Kant

---

15. For example, GA, II.3, p. 48. Numerous other references to the same occur throughout.
16. For a discussion of these attempts, including the reasons for which Kant ultimately rejected this strategy, see Henrich (1960, pp. 98–110).

attempted to exploit here was based upon the following idea: Whereas the concepts of the understanding order and unify the manifold of empirical intuition, the categorical imperative can be seen as effecting a unity, in the sense of logical consistency, among the subject's manifold desires and inclinations.

Although Kant ultimately rejected this strategy of deducing the moral law, it at least points out an interesting analogy that might be drawn between the two faculties with respect to their functions of unifying different aspects of experience. Fichte, however, is prevented from exploring this more plausible connection by the peculiar way in which he, in this early phase, conceives of practical reason and the unity it effects. This conception, which to some extent can still be found in the 1794 version of the *Wissenschaftslehre,* is articulated in the following excerpt from the "Eigene Meditationen":

> [In the preceding analysis] I and not-I are [in a certain respect] . . . *the same* . . . but they remain *two,* a duality. Shouldn't there also be numerical identity? I believe this to be the highest task of philosophy. It is only possible insofar as *things* come to be *adequate* determinations of our pure I, [that is, insofar as] justice prevails. This is the case with God.[17]

According to Fichte, then, the kind of unity sought by the faculty of practical reason is not a unity or consistency among the subject's various desires but a unity of the I with the not-I, or a unity of subject and object. More concretely, practical reason demands that the objective world be determined in such a way that it conforms to the requirements of the "pure" subject. This is to be understood simply as a rather abstract reformulation of Kant's own view, according to which practical reason requires that the moral subject act within the objective world and that this action be carried out in accord with norms that derive not from something external to the subject but, as Fichte puts it, from "our pure I."[18]

For the present we shall not quibble with Fichte's characterization of practical reason in terms of the subject's demand that the

17. GA, II.3, p. 132.
18. This aspect of Fichte's thought is presented in more detail in his 1794 lecture series entitled "The Vocation of the Scholar," where he redefines the categorical imperative in terms of the demand for harmony between oneself and the world, the I and the not-I. See GA, I.3, pp. 25–68, and SW, VI, pp. 291–346; these lectures are also translated by Breazeale in Fichte (1988, pp. 144–84).

object conform to its own essence. What interests us here is the fact that once the unity involved in the exercise of practical reason is understood in these terms, it becomes difficult to see how a plausible analogy could be drawn between the unity produced in the theoretical employment of reason and the unity for which practical reason supposedly strives. In the theoretical employment of reason, representations are unified in the sense that each belongs to a common subject, but this merely formal unity among the manifold elements of experience is quite distinct from the "numerical" unity of the I and not-I that is claimed to be involved in practical reason. The latter, on Fichte's view, requires a real transformation of the qualities of the objective world, an actual *determining* of the not-I in accord with the dictates of the subject's own being. It is fortunate, then, that Fichte soon abandons this particular strategy of deducing practical reason from the unity of apperception. In fact, Fichte's rejection of the latter as a starting point for his system can be regarded as the point that separates his presystematic phase from that of the *Wissenschaftslehre* proper. This important transition is clearly documented in the "Eigene Meditationen" in Fichte's explicit rejection of his initial starting point – the "merely formal principle" of the unity of apperception – and his subsequent instruction to himself to continue the search for a suitable starting point by "pursuing the unconditionedness of the I."[19]

The *Wissenschaftslehre* of 1794

The two main texts of 1794 that will interest us here are the *Foundation of the Entire Wissenschaftslehre* (henceforth, WL 1794) and its companion piece, *Concerning the Concept of the Wissenschaftslehre.*[20] Fichte intended the first text to be used as a handbook by the students attending his first academic lectures on the *Wissenschaftslehre,* and it is the main source for the doctrines of the 1794 system. The second work, which was written as a prospectus for the same lectures, is of value for its relatively clear presentation of the

19. "A spark of light: I get nowhere with the merely formal principle. . . . The I – can something be done here? – Pursue the unconditionedness of the I" *(Gehe der Unbedingtheit des Ich nach)* (GA, II.3, p. 48).
20. Since the *Foundation* was actually published in installments that appeared into 1795, it might be more accurate to refer to it as WL 1794–5. For the sake of simplicity, however, I shall use the shorter abbreviation.

general structure and method of Fichte's new system. The issue most central to Fichte's early conception of his philosophical system is the choice of a first principle, and it is in the discussion of the requirements of this starting point that this text provides the clearest insight into how Fichte understood the general aims of the *Wissenschaftslehre* in 1794.

In this period Fichte is still engaged in the project of deducing practical reason from a more basic principle that he believes will be able to serve as the starting point for all of philosophy. Yet the position of the WL 1794 differs from Fichte's presystematic phase in two ways. First, Fichte no longer attempts to deduce practical reason from the mere fact of the unity of consciousness; the path that his proof takes, rather, is to begin with a deduction of the principles of theoretical reason from the system's first principle and only then to deduce the principles of practical reason – this time by demonstrating them to be a necessary condition for the possibility, not of the unity of apperception, but of theoretical reason itself. Thus, the basic claim made here is that a faculty of theoretical reason is possible only on the presupposition of the capacity for practical reason, and in this sense, the former is grounded in the latter. The second and more important difference is Fichte's new conception of the *content* of the first principle that is to ground the whole of philosophy. Hence, what must concern us now is to understand each of these developments: What *is* Fichte's new principle in 1794, and by what path is philosophy led from this starting point to the rest of the system?

With regard to the former point Fichte's basic position is a familiar one to post-Cartesian philosophers: If philosophy is to provide us with genuine knowledge, then it must begin from a first principle that possesses absolute certainty in itself and independently of the system that is to follow from it. Such a principle cannot itself be proved (for then the premise of that proof would be the first principle) but must be in some way self-justifying.[21] And, if philosophy is to attain the status of a *Wissenschaft*, the first principle must be capable of conferring its certainty upon the propositions derived from it, so that what results is a system of knowledge in which each proposition possesses the same degree of certainty as the initial principle. Furthermore, Fichte conceives of this movement from the first principle to the rest of the system

21. SW, I, pp. 38–42.

as a chain of transcendental arguments in which each new proposition is deduced as a necessary condition for the possibility of the preceding one.[22] In other words, if an already established X can be shown to be impossible without the condition expressed in a new proposition Y, then Y must be accorded the same degree of certainty originally attributed to X.

Although the general structure of the system that Fichte intends to construct is relatively clear, the content of the claims actually put forth by the WL 1794 is notoriously obscure. Nowhere is this more evident, nor of greater consequence, than in the case of the system's first principle. There is, of course, no difficulty in identifying the proposition that is to serve as first principle: "The I originally and unconditionally posits its own existence."[23] What is less clear is what this principle is intended to mean. I shall try to show that part of this obscurity is due to the fact that in the WL 1794 Fichte himself is still confused about the precise content of his first principle. This confusion manifests itself in a basic conflict between the content of the first principle as it is articulated in Section 1 of the WL 1794 and the way in which Fichte actually uses this principle throughout the work, especially in the transition from theoretical to practical reason.

As we have already seen, in 1793 Fichte turned from his initial starting point of the unity of apperception and proceeded to search for a new first principle by investigating what he calls the "unconditionedness" *(Unbedingtheit)* of the I. This decision, recorded in the "Eigene Meditationen," suggests that the principle with which the WL 1794 begins is intended, above all, to give expression to the "unconditioned" nature of the I. Indeed, the language of the first section of the WL 1794 seems to bear out this hypothesis, for in discussing his first principle, Fichte invariably uses expressions such as 'self-grounded', 'absolute', and 'unconditionally posited' *(schlechthin gesetzt)* to characterize the I.[24] Our

22. SW, I, p. 446. Although this passage dates from a later period (1797), it applies equally well to the 1794 *Wissenschaftslehre*.

23. "Das Ich setzt ursprünglich schlechthin sein eigenes Sein" (SW, I, p. 98). The precise translation of *schlechthin* is notoriously problematic. I have chosen 'unconditionally' to emphasize the unconditioned nature of the subject's self-positing. Other possibilities include 'unqualifiedly', 'absolutely' (Heath and Lachs, 1982), 'simply' (Breazeale, 1988). At GA, IV.2, p. 31, Fichte clarifies a bit what the term *schlechthin* is intended to convey: "The I posits itself *unconditionally (schlechthin)*, i.e., without any mediation."

24. SW, I, pp. 95–6.

task, then, is to uncover the sense in which the WL 1794 asserts the subject to be absolute or unconditioned.

It is at this point that we encounter one of the most fundamental and controversial issues within Fichte scholarship: What is it about the subject that Fichte means to express in his very first principle? At its most general level, the controversy consists in the question of whether the notion of the unconditioned, self-positing I involves a claim about the *practical* nature of the subject, or whether it is to be understood as a starting point with a purely *theoretical* content.[25] According to the former interpretation, Fichte's first principle is above all a statement about the *moral* nature of the subject and embodies a claim concerning the subject's capacity for practical freedom. The subject, on this view, is "unconditioned" in the sense that, unlike objects, which are always subject to the conditions of causal determination, the I is capable of *self*-determination. According to the latter interpretation, 'self-positing' denotes a feature of the I that is appropriately described as "unconditioned" but that, to use Kant's distinction, belongs to the domain of theoretical rather than practical reason. Proponents of this reading tend to see the first principle as expressing a doctrine borrowed from or developed out of Kant's account of pure apperception in the first *Critique*. The subject matter of the principle is characterized by these interpreters in a variety of ways, by means of such formulations as the "formal identity of self-consciousness," the "immediate self-certainty" of the I, the "'I am I' of pure self-consciousness," and simply the Cartesian "I am."[26] Although there is some disagreement over the precise content of the starting point, what is common to all of these interpretations is the view that the first principle itself makes no direct claim about the ethical or practical aspects of subjectivity.

According to the position that I shall develop in this chapter, there is no way of deciding between these two interpretations as long as one restricts oneself to the text of the WL 1794. This is because in different parts of this work Fichte unwittingly and

25. This is the same question addressed by Peter Baumanns, although he characterizes the two alternatives as "ethical–anthropological" and "transcendental–phenomenological," respectively. See Baumanns (1972, 1974).
26. Baumanns (1974, pp. 149, 185, 12). This line of interpretation is represented by an otherwise extremely diverse group of commentators that includes Lauth (1964, pp. 253–85), Pippin (1988, pp. 74–96), Henrich (1982, pp. 15–53), and Wildt (1982).

inconsistently subscribes to *both* versions of his starting point. In order to see more clearly how Fichte operates with two distinct conceptions of his first principle, it will be necessary to examine the first substantive account of this principle given in the opening section of the WL 1794.[27] In this portion of the text, where one of Fichte's main concerns is to emphasize the apodicticity of his starting point, it is possible to establish conclusively that the first principle is intended as a purely "theoretical" starting point that can be fully grasped without reference to the moral or practical nature of the I.[28] Apart from this general conclusion, though, what specifically is meant to be asserted by this principle?

It is tempting to conclude from Section 1 that what Fichte intends to express in his first principle is simply Descartes's "I am." Apart from the fact that this starting point would cohere well with his Cartesian understanding of the nature of a first principle, there are a number of passages that, by emphasizing the *ich bin,* suggest such an interpretation.[29] Although the subject's certainty of its own existence as a conscious being is of great importance to Fichte's first principle, it is not this self-certainty alone that is at issue. The unconditioned nature of the I, rather, is expressed in the following claim: "The I *posits itself,* and it *exists* by virtue of this mere self-positing."[30] A full account of Fichte's doctrine of the

27. SW, I, pp. 91–101.
28. Apart from the argumentation provided later, there is a considerable amount of straightforward textual evidence to support this conclusion. Most importantly, there is simply no reference in the first section of Part I to the subject's practical capacity. More specifically, one could point to Fichte's remark at the end of this section (SW, I, p. 99) that Kant himself *in his deduction of the categories* (and, hence, in his account of *theoretical* consciousness) implicitly referred to the same principle that is taken by the *Wissenschaftslehre* as the first principle of all of philosophy. As I shall try to show, it is only in the next phase of Fichte's development, the period of 1797–9, that Fichte explicitly comes to regard his first principle as having a practical as well as a theoretical content. Although Baumanns (1972) argues forcefully for the ethical interpretation of the WL 1794, most of the textual evidence that he cites in favor of his position is taken from the 1797 introductions and then read back into the position of 1794. In his second book (1974) Baumanns comes very close to endorsing my own interpretation, insofar as he emphasizes the dual nature of Fichte's original starting point and insofar as his detailed analysis of Section 1 of the WL 1794 confirms that Fichte's own arguments here (to their detriment, according to Baumanns) concern exclusively theoretical subjectivity. See especially pp. 174–5, 185.
29. See numerous references to the "I am" and its connection to the *Tathandlung* throughout SW, I, pp. 94–9.
30. "Das Ich *setzt sich selbst,* und es *ist,* vermöge dieses blossen Setzens durch sich selbst" (SW, I, p. 96).

self-positing subject would lead us too far afield here, but the specific point in which we are presently interested is clarified in a subsequent passage: "*What* was I before I came to self-consciousness? The natural answer to this question is: *I* did not exist at all, for I was not an I. The I exists only insofar as it is conscious of itself."[31]

This passage makes clear that Fichte uses the notion of self-positing to refer to a particular kind of *self-consciousness* and that his characterization of the I as absolute or unconditioned is to be understood as consisting in the claim that the subject has no existence apart from this self-awareness. The I is "self-grounded" in the sense that its act of self-intuition constitutes its being. Although we shall investigate this fundamental claim in greater detail in the following chapter, for our present purpose it is important to note the relatively modest nature of Fichte's understanding of the subject's "unconditionedness." Contrary to popular notions about the WL 1794, Fichte is not claiming here that the I is absolute in the sense that it is the cause of, or to be identified with, the whole of reality. Furthermore, the first principle, as it is explicated in the beginning of the WL 1794, cannot plausibly be said to possess any *immediate* implications concerning the practical or moral nature of the subject. In other words, the principle of the self-positing subject found in Section 1 is manifestly not, nor was it intended to be, a principle about the subject's capacity for practical freedom or moral autonomy. Even though Fichte characterizes the subject's self-positing as an *act,* there are no apparent grounds for concluding that his first principle is, for this reason alone, relevant to real, practical activity as well. This point is best illustrated by recalling that for Kant, too, theoretical self-consciousness consisted in a spontaneous act on the part of the subject. Yet this capacity – the ability to recognize my representations as belonging to me – does not imply in any direct way that the subject is also free in the practical sense of being able to determine its own will in accord with the dictates of practical reason. This is not to say that the WL 1794 is unconcerned with practical reason and its relation to the theoretical realm. On the

31. SW, I, p. 97. A more systematic analysis of the notion of the absolute, self-positing subject, including the doctrine of the *Tathandlung,* will be postponed until Chapter 3. For the present we are concerned only with the general nature of the WL 1794's first principle and the role it will play in the deduction of practical reason.

contrary, the task of proving practical reason remains a primary objective of this work, as evidenced by Fichte's claim in Section 5 of Part III to have done precisely this.[32] The crucial point, however, is that Fichte does not regard the existence of practical reason as already contained within the first principle itself. Whereas the Gebhard review envisioned an immediate move from the unity of apperception to the existence of practical reason, the path traversed in the WL 1794 is considerably less direct. It is the course of this "deduction" of practical reason to which we now turn.

The general structure of Fichte's intended proof is clear enough: A proof of practical reason "is possible only by showing that reason cannot itself be theoretical if it is not practical, that no intelligence in the human being is possible unless it also possesses a practical faculty."[33] Thus, Fichte will endeavor to prove the existence of practical reason by showing that such a faculty is a necessary condition for the possibility of theoretical reason. This strategy is consistent with our previous characterization of Fichte's method as consisting in a continuous series of transcendental arguments that moves from a particular feature of consciousness to the conditions of the same. Although the account of theoretical reason will precede that of practical reason in order of exposition, this strategy actually implies a *primacy* of practical reason over theoretical reason in the sense that the latter is shown to be grounded in, or conditioned by, the former.

Having pointed out the kind of argument that is envisioned, our task becomes one of understanding how Fichte intends to show that theoretical reason requires a faculty of practical reason as its condition. Since the strategy for this proof is embedded in the very structure of the work, it will first be necessary to note briefly the overall organization of the WL 1794. After a first section, which elucidates the three fundamental principles of the *Wissenschafts-lehre* as a whole, the text is divided into two main parts, of which the first is devoted to theoretical knowledge and the second to the "science of the practical." Unlike Kant in the first two *Critiques*, Fichte does not intend to provide two separate and unconnected accounts of the two forms of reason. Rather, Fichte's position here is that there is an important continuity between the analyses of theoretical and practical reason and that the existence of the latter can be proved by articulating the nature of this connection.

32. SW, I, p. 264.   33. SW, I, p. 264.

Hence, the argument behind Fichte's attempt to prove practical reason in the WL 1794 will be found in the transition from the analysis of theoretical reason in Part II to the treatment of practical reason in Part III. The manner in which this transition is to proceed is laid out clearly near the end of Part I:[34] The analysis of theoretical reason will result in a fundamental contradiction that cannot be eradicated by remaining within the domain of theoretical reason alone, and the necessity of postulating a faculty of practical reason will be demonstrated by showing that it alone is capable of resolving that contradiction. The first step in understanding Fichte's argument, then, is to uncover the contradiction that allegedly inheres in the account of theoretical reason.

The primary aim of the theoretical part of the WL 1794 is to give an account of the features of theoretical consciousness that, whenever possible, explains those features as a consequence of the subject's own nature rather than as dependent upon something external to the subject. Whereas for Kant the subject's activity provided the formal elements of empirical knowledge, the content of that knowledge was understood as resulting from the object's ability to "affect" a subject that, in this relation to its object, is merely passive. It is Fichte's aim to go beyond this position and claim that the subject plays an active role, not merely with respect to the forms of cognition, but in generating the content of sensation as well. It is this position that is expressed in Fichte's well-known doctrine of the *Anstoß* (check) and that constitutes the end point of the theoretical portion of the WL 1794. Fichte invokes the notion of an *Anstoß* in order to explain the possibility of representation and, more specifically, to give an account of what Kant called the "matter of sensation." The matter of sensation is explained here, not in terms of a thing's activity upon the self, but rather as the result of an "infinite" activity on the part of the subject that is "checked," or blocked, by the inert, wholly passive *Anstoß* and then reflected back to the subject. The reflection that the subject's activity undergoes is intended to explain why the perceiving subject normally takes what is actually its own activity to be affection by an external, independent thing. Although our present concerns do not require that we retrace the tortuous path by which Fichte claims to have arrived at this position, it is impor-

34. SW, I, p. 115.

tant that we understand the basic claim underlying the doctrine of
the *Anstoß:* Although it is possible to go farther than Kant in
accounting for the characteristics of knowledge in terms of the
subject's own activity, there remains an element of that knowledge
which is fundamentally irreducible to the subject's spontaneity. In
other words, it is ultimately impossible to eradicate every trace of
the nonsubjective (the "not-I") from an account of theoretical
knowledge. Even though Fichte has reduced the role of Kant's
thing in itself to that of a mere check upon the subject's otherwise
unlimited activity, representation is nonetheless impossible without this *Anstoß*, and therefore the theoretical subject is irremedia-
bly dependent upon something other than itself, that is, upon a
not-I.

It is precisely this dependence of the I upon the not-I that, in
Fichte's view, generates a contradiction within his system. More
specifically, Fichte's claim is that philosophy cannot be satisfied
with this account of theoretical reason, because the dependence of
the I required by this account conflicts with the first principle of
the *Wissenschaftslehre*. This is important for our account of Fichte's
starting point, for it allows us to determine the sense in which
Fichte, outside of Part I of the WL 1794, actually construes his
first principle. Indeed, in the transition to practical reason Fichte
characterizes this principle as asserting that "the I, in all of its
determinations, is to be unconditionally posited by itself and,
therefore, completely independent of any possible not-I."[35] The
import of the first principle here, it would seem, is to assert that
the essence of the I lies in its self-sufficiency, that it is the nature
of the I to be completely independent of the not-I or, in other
words, to be wholly self-determining and undetermined in any
way by its object. And, if the first principle is understood in this
way, it becomes apparent why Fichte regards it as conflicting with
the theoretical subject's ultimate dependence upon an *Anstoß*.

The second step in the deduction of practical reason consists in
showing that a faculty of practical reason can eliminate the conflict between theoretical philosophy and the system's starting
point. The contradiction between the radical independence of the

---

35. SW, I, p. 249. See also GA, I.2, pp. 150–1, where Fichte states clearly that
the contradiction at issue is one between the *results* of the theoretical *Wissenschaftslehre* and the system's "highest and absolutely first principle."

I that is asserted in the first principle and the dependence of the I required by theoretical reason is to be resolved in the following manner: " . . . the *dependence* of the I as intelligence [i.e., as theoretical subject] must be eliminated. This is conceivable only under the condition *that this hitherto unknown not-I* to which the *Anstoß* is attributed . . . *be determined by the I itself.*"[36] In other words, the requirements of the first principle would be satisfied if the subject could be regarded as having determined, or caused, the *Anstoß* required for theoretical knowledge. For in this case, that upon which the I is dependent within theoretical knowledge, the not-I, would be nothing more than a product of the I itself. By creating the object upon which it, as theoretical subject, depends, the I would remain wholly self-determining, even though that self-determination would be indirect in the sense that it would be mediated by what appears to be a not-I. Yet this attempt to resolve the conflict between theoretical reason and the first principle must itself be revised, for it too engenders a contradiction, this time with the *Wissenschaftslehre*'s second principle: "A not-I is unqualifiedly posited in opposition to the I."[37] In this context the second principle is to be understood as asserting the essential finitude and limitedness of the subject inherent in the claim that the I requires a relation to something radically different from itself in order for it to be an I. If the second principle is understood in this sense, the solution just sketched becomes untenable. The I cannot simply be the cause of the *Anstoß*, for then there would be no not-I in the true sense. All difference between subject and object would be apparent rather than real, and the claim articulated in the system's second principle would be negated.

At this point it becomes clear that the contradiction at issue is grounded in the basic conflict between the first two principles of the WL 1794 and that, as Fichte explicitly says here, this conflict stems from two necessary, yet seemingly opposed characterizations of the self as "infinite and unlimited," on the one hand, and "finite and limited," on the other.[38] Thus, the problem to be solved by an appeal to practical reason is one of reconciling the I's "absolute" nature with its fundamental finitude, that is, with the fact that it cannot exist as an I without an "other." What must be found is a way of understanding the activity of the I in such a way that it remains "absolute" without at the same time annihilating

36. SW, I, p. 249.   37. SW, I, p. 104.   38. SW, I, p. 255.

the not-I. Fichte attempts to fulfill this requirement by introducing the notion of "striving" *(Streben)*. Instead of postulating the relation between I and not-I to be one of complete determination of the latter by the former, Fichte ascribes to the I "merely a tendency, a striving toward determination [of the not-I]."[39] The goal of this striving is the subject's absolute independence from its object in the sense that the determinations of the latter are wholly dependent upon the I: "The I is to be absolutely independent, whereas everything is to be dependent upon the I. Hence, what is demanded is the conformity (*Uebereinstimmung*) of the object with the I."[40] Thus, the striving subject is "absolute" with respect to the *goal* of its striving (i.e., insofar as it endeavors to make the not-I conform to its own essence), but the point of characterizing the I's activity as a "mere" striving is to accommodate the fact that the I can never attain its goal of complete independence from its object. In other words, the principle of striving is intended to take into account the ineradicable finitude of the subject expressed in the second principle, while still attributing to the I an "absolute" quality that, by the end of the *Wissenschaftslehre,* is understood, not as a *fact* about the subject, but as a *demand* that the I makes upon itself and its world.

The third and final step of the deduction occurs in the identification of the subject's striving with a faculty of practical reason. The basic idea behind this move is already familiar to us from the characterization of practical reason in the "Eigene Meditationen." Fichte's conclusion in the WL 1794 that the I is characterized by an infinite striving to make the not-I conform to itself is to be understood as nothing more than the claim that the I is subject to the moral law. This step of the argument becomes comprehensible if we regard the moral law as demanding that the subject act upon the objective world in order to make it conform to an imperative that is given by the subject to itself in accord only with the principles of its own nature. Therefore, for Fichte, deducing the necessity of such a striving is tantamount to proving the reality of a faculty of practical reason: "The demand that everything conform to the I, that all reality is to be unqualifiedly posited by the I, is the demand of what one calls practical reason."[41]

A number of objections could be raised against this proof, but what is of concern to us here is not so much the validity of Fichte's

39. SW, I, p. 261.   40. SW, I, p. 260.   41. SW, I, p. 263.

argument as the general outline of the deduction and its implications for an understanding of the *Wissenschaftslehre*'s first principle. As we saw earlier, the conflict that necessitated the introduction of practical reason arose because the I's dependence upon the object – a dependence that could never be eliminated within the theoretical realm – contradicted the system's first principle. Yet in order for such a conflict to arise it is necessary to interpret the first principle in a way that is blatantly at odds with Fichte's characterization of that principle in Part I of the WL 1794. In the transition to practical reason, the principle "the I unconditionally posits itself" is taken to mean something like "the I demands complete independence from the not-I" or "the I must be wholly self-determined and completely undetermined by anything external to itself." Yet this construal of the first principle obviously constitutes a shift in meaning with respect to the position laid out in Part I. For there the I's "self-positing" seemed to refer not to the subject's quest for practical "self-sufficiency," but rather to an alleged characteristic of the theoretical subject, namely, that the subject has no existence apart from its own activity of self-awareness. Thus, there is nothing in Part I of the WL 1794 that could justify interpreting the first principle in the sense required for the deduction of the I's absolute striving. Moreover, if this interpretation were given to the first principle, it is difficult to see how that principle could satisfy Fichte's unambiguous demand in the 1794 system for an apodictic starting point.

For these reasons we must conclude that the proof of practical reason attempted in the WL 1794 fails due to a fundamental inconsistency in the employment of its first principle. In Part I Fichte claims to begin with what is allegedly an absolutely certain starting point derived from a consideration of the phenomenon of theoretical self-consciousness. In Part III, however, his aim of deducing practical reason requires him to ascribe to that principle a meaning that is quite distinct from its original sense. In effect, the first principle here, in asserting the I's need to be completely self-sufficient and undetermined by any object, takes on a *practical* significance that, though useful to a proof of practical reason, cannot measure up to the standards of apodicticity espoused by Fichte elsewhere. In adopting the practical version of his first principle, Fichte necessarily surrenders the certainty of that principle and thereby dissolves the very foundation upon which the truth of his system, including its proof of practical reason, was to be based. Although Fichte never explicitly points out this basic inconsistency in the WL 1794, the focus of his work during the period immediately following strongly suggests that he eventually came to recognize this very problem. For, as we shall see, one of the central preoccupations of these later texts is the attempt to clarify both the content and epistemological status of the principle of the self-positing subject and, in doing so, to re-think the relation between theoretical and practical reason.

The system of 1797–9

In 1797 Fichte published the first chapter of what he intended to be a second and improved version of his philosophical system under the name "Attempt at a New Presentation of the *Wissenschaftslehre.*" There is no doubt that the philosophical community's widespread misunderstanding and ridicule of the first version played a major role in convincing Fichte that a "new presentation" of his system was necessary. But it would be wrong to conclude that Fichte's sole motive for composing this second version was simply to present more clearly the same doctrines put forth in the first. In addition to their greater clarity, the writings of 1797–9 bear witness to substantive developments in Fichte's thought, especially with respect to the choice of a first principle and to the relation between theoretical and practical reason. The texts of this period that address these issues most directly are the two introductions to the *Wissenschaftslehre* published in 1797 in Fichte's own *Philosophisches Journal.* The purpose of these new introductions, according to Fichte, is to prepare and orient the reader by providing a "description of the *perspective* from which the transcendental philosopher beholds all knowledge."[42] They are introductory in the sense that they aim to lead the uninitiated reader to the point at which entry into the system proper can be gained. Since this entry point is nothing other than the system's first principle, the primary goal of the two introductions is to enhance the reader's ability to comprehend and accept that founding principle. What we can expect from Fichte's new introductions, then, is a more detailed account than we have seen thus far of the sense in which philosophy's first principle is to be understood. Moreover, the simple fact that Fichte now deems such a propaedeutic to be

42. SW, I, pp. 33–4, my emphasis.

necessary for an understanding of that principle suggests a fundamental revision of his earlier notion of a self-evident, universally
recognized starting point.

The most significant development in Fichte's position consists
in the fact that there is no longer any ambiguity with respect
to the practical nature of the system's first principle. The self-
consciousness from which the *Wissenschaftslehre* begins is now
explicitly and consistently described as a "feeling of [one's] freedom and absolute self-sufficiency,"[43] and numerous passages make
clear that Fichte means here a consciousness not just of the spontaneity of the theoretical subject but of practical freedom as well.
This self-consciousness is also characterized as an awareness
of the "absolute self-activity of the I," of one's "independence of
everything outside of oneself," and, further, as the awareness of
oneself "not as determined by things, but rather as determining
them."[44] These formulations are easily recognized as essentially
identical to those used by Fichte to characterize the absolute
nature of the I in the later sections of the WL 1794 where he was
concerned with the deduction of a faculty of practical reason.
Although these expressions remain rather vague, they are apparently intended to assert both the importance and the possibility of
the subject's achievement of genuine autonomy through real,
practical self-determination. For the moment it is unnecessary to
determine more precisely the notion of autonomy at work in this
characterization of the subject; what is of greater interest is that
here, for the first time, Fichte explicitly acknowledges that his
point of departure is also itself a *practical* principle. In other words,
Fichte gives us to understand that the principle of the self-positing
subject that founds the *Wissenschaftslehre* is, at least in part, a
statement about the practical nature of the subject, where 'practical' refers not merely to ideal "activities" of consciousness but to
the subject's interaction with and determination of real objects.
This explicit emphasis upon the practical nature of the first principle is undoubtedly intended to resolve the confusion surrounding the precise meaning of that principle in the WL 1794. In this
context Fichte's move in 1797 is to be understood as a rejection of
the purely theoretical starting point of the opening section of the

---

43. "[Ein] Gefühl ihrer Freiheit und absoluten Selbständigkeit" (SW, I, p. 433).
44. SW, I, pp. 471, 433, 467.

WL 1794 in favor of the fuller, more substantial interpretation of the first principle prominent in the later sections of that work, where the "absolute" nature of the I was defined in terms of its essential need for complete self-determination. Furthermore, this choice most likely proceeds from a realization that the narrower, merely theoretical starting point will never enable him to arrive at a deduction of a faculty of practical reason.

This shift in Fichte's conception of his first principle raises two serious questions with implications for his most basic philosophical goals. First, and most obvious, what becomes of Fichte's project of proving practical reason by showing it to be one of the conditions for the possibility of theoretical reason? How can such a proof be carried out if Fichte *begins* with the practical subject? We shall return to this important question later, after we have considered the second problem, which is closely related: What remains of Fichte's previous account of the requirements of a well-founded philosophical system? Can this new starting point measure up to the standard of self-evident certainty that Fichte espoused in 1794? Is it not at least possible that the subject's sense of itself as free with respect to the objective world might be illusory? It was undoubtedly this very problem that was responsible for the second major change in Fichte's understanding of his first principle in 1797: the abandonment of the view that the starting point of idealism is a self-evident, universally recognized proposition. This development finds expression in Fichte's characterization of that principle, in contrast to his view of 1794, as a "belief" *(Glaube)* and in the related claim that the justification of that starting point is not grounded in purely speculative reason but in a choice that is based upon "inclination and interest."[45]

This last claim arises in the context of Fichte's discussion of what he takes to be the only two systems of philosophy possible: dogmatism and his own system, idealism. The former, which Fichte holds to be best represented by Spinozism,[46] takes the thing in itself—or "substance"—as its point of departure and from there attempts to give an account of all of reality, including subjectivity. Such a system, on Fichte's view, is obligated to understand all of

---

45. SW, I, pp. 466, 433.
46. Perhaps it should be stated explicitly that we are concerned here not with the actual views of Spinoza but with Fichte's understanding of the nature of "dogmatism."

the features of consciousness as effects of the actions of external things upon the subject. Thus, even the subject's seemingly free choices must be explained as resulting in some complex way from causal determination by things rather than as instances of genuine self-determination. The strategy of idealism, in contrast, is to begin with what it regards as the essential nature of the subject – the "self-sufficiency of the I" – and upon this basis to explain all of experience, including the necessary features of the objective world. What is of interest to us in this discussion of the conflict between idealism and dogmatism is the new way in which Fichte understands the kind and degree of certainty that can be attributed to his first principle and to the system that follows from it. The crux of Fichte's view is expressed in his admission that idealism cannot "directly" refute dogmatism, as well as in his celebrated dictum that "the kind of philosophy one chooses depends upon what kind of person one is."[47]

Fichte's position here has often been taken to imply a kind of radical relativism, according to which the espousal of a particular philosophy is a fundamentally personal and subjective choice that can ultimately be based upon nothing more than an unfounded preference for one view of the world over another. In what follows I shall argue that this is not in fact Fichte's view and that this frequently cited claim applies only to a specific case, namely, to one's initial philosophical orientation before engaging in any systematic reflection upon that perspective.[48] Since on Fichte's account it is each system's starting point that embodies the general orientation of that philosophy, his position here can be translated into a claim about the epistemological status of philosophy's first principle: With regard to the *initial* choice of a first principle, before one has considered the actual systems that follow from different principles, reason in its purely speculative function can provide us with no basis for preferring one starting point over the other. This should not be taken to imply that the two candidates for the role of first principle express propositions that, although distinct in content, are both apodictically certain. This could not be the case, since Fichte views the two principles as contradictory.

---

47. SW, I, p. 434. See also p. 429: "Keines dieser beiden Systeme kann das entgegengesetzte direkt widerlegen."
48. I argue more thoroughly for this interpretation later. My position here is based upon two detailed discussions of the 1797 introductions, one by Breazeale (1988, pp. 97–123), the other by Baumanns (1974, pp. 122–38).

Hence, it must be that from a speculative point of view *neither* can be regarded as apodictically certain. Indeed, this conclusion is borne out by Fichte's statements in the first introduction that the dogmatist does not acknowledge the truth of idealism's first principle and is even prevented from doing so because of "the kind of person" he is. This claim becomes more comprehensible when we recall that Fichte now regards his first principle as an assertion of the essentially practical, autonomous nature of the subject; those individuals who do not believe in their own capacity for real self-determination will be unable to assent to the *Wissenschaftslehre*'s starting point. By admitting that there are rational human beings who are incapable of recognizing the truth of that starting point, Fichte commits himself to the view that his own first principle, in isolation from the system that it engenders, does not have the kind of self-evidence possessed by such statements as *"A = A"* or "I am." What this implies for Fichte is that even the vivid and immediate sense of freedom possessed by those characters most suited to the study of idealism cannot be taken as certain *knowledge* of that freedom. The most that such a "natural" idealist could be said to have prior to systematic philosophical reflection is a strong *belief* in her freedom. Furthermore, what brings one to believe in that feeling – that is, to regard it as more than illusory – is not theoretical rationality but the subject's interest in its own autonomy.

Hence, the development that Fichte's conception of his starting point undergoes in the system of 1797–9 can be understood in terms of two significant changes. The first of these concerns the content of that starting point and consists in the fact that the principle of self-positing is no longer understood as a statement only about the self-consciousness of the theoretical subject but as a principle that also asserts the subject's capacity for practical self-determination. The second change is that the first principle no longer expresses an absolutely certain fact about the subject but is accorded instead the status of a belief that is grounded in one's interest in one's own autonomy. Characterizing Fichte's development in this way, however, leads us back to a problem that was raised earlier, for, taken together, these two revisions seem to pose insuperable obstacles to Fichte's goal of devising a more substantial proof of practical reason than Kant was able to provide. First, it is difficult to see how Fichte could now be in a position to surpass Kant's own appeal to practical belief as the ultimate justification for freedom. For in light of his new conception of the

Wissenschaftslehre, the system that was to furnish a proof of practical reason now rests upon a first principle that is itself founded upon a kind of practical belief. Furthermore, it is clear that the strategy of such a proof can no longer be conceived of as a transcendental argument that begins with an indisputable principle and deduces practical reason as a necessary condition of that starting point. For now, we are told, the first principle itself already asserts what for Fichte has always been the crucial thing to be *established* by a proof of practical reason, namely, the subject's capacity for genuine self-determination. If we take seriously Fichte's claims about the practical import of his first principle, it is no longer clear what remains for a proof of practical reason to demonstrate.

It would seem, then, that Fichte's new conception of his first principle would require him to abandon his project of providing a proof of practical reason. His actual response, however, is not to give up this basic goal, but only to pursue it along a different route. In other words, there remains an important sense in which Fichte regards his system of 1797–9 as providing a philosophical grounding for the principles of practical reason. To understand this aspect of his new system it will be necessary to return to Fichte's comparison of idealism and dogmatism and, more specifically, to his claim that the choice between them ultimately depends upon one's character. We have already noted that this point has often been understood as a thoroughly relativistic claim that would rule out the possibility of a rational choice between the two rival systems. While it is easy to recognize the textual basis for this interpretation, it is demonstrably not the view Fichte intended to uphold. In the section immediately following the passage at issue, Fichte goes on to claim that idealism's superiority to its rival *can* be demonstrated but that this decisive proof can be had only when one is in a position to view the results of both attempts to construct a philosophical system. The inadequacy of dogmatism consists in the fact that, by starting from the thing itself, it will never be able to arrive at an account of the *consciousness* of things and therefore will prove incapable of constructing a single, all-encompassing system. Idealism, on the other hand, will prove to be successful – the *Wissenschaftslehre* itself is to be concrete evidence of this fact – in establishing a single chain of connected arguments that deduce a complete catalogue of the features of subjective and objective experience. The decisive strength of idealism, then, lies in its ability to achieve *completeness,* and it is precisely this feature that Fichte regards not only as a proof of its overall superiority to dogmatism but as a confirmation of the truth of its starting point as well. Hence, the *belief* in the subject's freedom with which the *Wissenschaftslehre* begins is ultimately *verified (bewährt)* by its ability to serve as the foundation for the only truly systematic and complete philosophy achievable.[49]

It is not difficult to see that the kind of argument that is to prove the reality of practical reason in the system of 1797–9 is fundamentally different from Fichte's earlier strategies for achieving the same goal. Fichte no longer conceives of his proof as a particular argument that could be reconstructed outside the context of the system itself, nor does it correspond to a single step within that system, such as the transition from theoretical to practical philosophy in the WL 1794. Rather, it is now the success of the system as a whole that constitutes the "proof" of practical reason. More precisely, it is the system's capacity to comprehend the whole of experience that demonstrates the truth of its initial, merely hypothetical assertion of freedom and thereby delivers what Fichte has been looking for all along – decisive proof of the subject's capacity for practical self-determination.

Thus, it is clear that in 1797 Fichte is still pursuing one version of his goal of proving the reality of practical reason, but in the meantime, what has become of his attempt to demonstrate the unity of theoretical and practical reason? The answer to this question is complex, but the upshot of what I shall argue is that Fichte's system of 1797–9 continues to assert the unity of the two faculties in the second (and weaker) sense distinguished in Chapter 1 (i.e., both are unified within a single system that proceeds from a common first principle) but that his new position also allows him to maintain the unity of reason in a deeper sense as well (the third sense outlined, namely, that both have the same internal "structure").

One interesting consequence of Fichte's new strategy is that the task of proving practical reason merges completely with his aim of systematizing the disparate elements of Critical Philosophy into a coherent whole. This means that by 1797 a single desideratum, the achievement of systematicity (which includes bringing theoretical and practical reason into a single system), is seen as the solution both to the problem of proving practical reason and to the

49. SW, I, p. 466.

issue of the unity of reason in its weaker form. In a sense, this convergence of strategies represents nothing new, since from the very beginning Fichte regarded the remedy for the lack of unity between theoretical and practical reason as inseparably bound up with his more general project of constructing a single unified system of philosophy. But it is possible to pinpoint even more precisely the aspect of systematicity around which these two tasks converge in the system of 1797–9. The preceding account of the early versions of Fichte's system has pointed out how the single most important element of the quest for a proof of practical reason came to be the search for an appropriate first principle, one that would permit a deduction of the principles of both theoretical and practical reason. We shall see that the selection of a suitable first principle holds the key to the unification of theoretical and practical reason as well and, moreover, that this is true for *both* the weaker and stronger versions of that project.

Even in Fichte's initial conception of his system, as laid out in the Gebhard review, the attempt to demonstrate the unity of reason was closely connected to the issue of a first principle. Although the precise details of his argument remained unarticulated, the general strategy of the project was clear enough to indicate the sense in which that early system understood theoretical and practical reason to be unitary: The principles of each were to be deduced from a single starting point and within a single, connected system. More specifically, Fichte envisioned a transcendental argument that would reveal how both theoretical and practical reason constituted necessary conditions for the possibility of the formal unity of consciousness. In this way, Kant's strategy in the first *Critique* – his demonstration of the necessity of the categories as a condition for the unity of consciousness in general – was to be extended to include the principles of practical reason as well.

There is indeed a sense in which the successful execution of this plan could be said to demonstrate an important connection between theoretical and practical reason. What such an argument could claim to show is the necessity of positing both faculties, as well as the possibility of deducing each of them within the framework of a single system. Although the latter achievement can be understood as establishing a sort of unity of theoretical and practical reason (in the second sense), it clearly does not demonstrate the deeper unity (of the third sense) alluded to in Kant's expression of hope in the *Groundwork* for a future account of theoretical and practical reason that would show them to be, not two distinct faculties, but merely two "applications" of a single faculty of reason.[50] Such an account would presumably have to point out a more intimate affinity between theoretical and practical reason, an affinity that would be somehow internal to the structure of each and that would constitute the "identity" of the two. Whatever form such an account might actually take, it is clear that Fichte's early conceptions of his system do not go very far toward demonstrating the unity of reason in this stronger sense.

Although Fichte rejects the specific strategy of the Gebhard review early on, he never abandons the goal of accounting for both theoretical and practical reason within a single system, and for this reason his project during this period can be seen as upholding the unity of reason in the weaker of the two senses. Beyond this, however, I shall try to show that the developments undergone by the *Wissenschaftslehre* in response to the difficulties of proving practical reason enable Fichte in the system of 1797–9 to assert the essential unity of theoretical and practical reason in a more substantial sense than was possible in either of the two earlier phases. As I have suggested, the key to this new possibility lies in Fichte's revised conception of his first principle. The crucial point to be recalled here is that by 1797, in contrast to his earlier positions, Fichte had come to see that the *Wissenschaftslehre*'s first principle must itself include some kind of assertion about the practical nature of the I if it is to succeed in founding a system that encompasses both the theoretical and practical aspects of reason. At the same time, however, if it is to engender a unitary system, the starting point must be a *single* principle, as opposed to a compound that simply conjoins a theoretical principle with a practical one. It would seem, then, that the role of the first principle must be to point to a feature of consciousness that is central to and shared by both theoretical and practical reason. Thus, it would be reasonable to expect that the key to understanding the unity of reason is to be found already within that principle itself.

This point, however, provides us with only an abstract understanding of the role that Fichte's first principle is to perform in articulating the essential unity of theoretical and practical reason. What is missing from our account is a specific analysis of what the

50. GMS, p. 391.

principle of self-positing asserts about the subject. It is one thing to understand why Fichte, given his general goals, lays down certain formal requirements for his first principle; it is quite another matter to envision how these requirements are actually to be met by a particular principle. The rest of this study will be concerned with filling in the details of this undertaking, and in the remaining pages of the present chapter I shall attempt to sketch out the basic features of what I take to represent the guiding force behind the mature form of Fichte's project.

The central question that faces us is: How are we to understand Fichte's claim that his first principle possesses both a practical and a theoretical import while remaining a *single* principle? In order to answer this question we shall turn first to a letter written by Fichte to Reinhold after the publication of the WL 1794. Of most concern to us is a passage in which Fichte attempts to clear up some of the obscurity surrounding his first principle by articulating the disagreement that he believes to exist among Kant, Reinhold, and himself:

> In my view our disagreement consists in the following: If you [in your *Elementar-Philosophie*] have laid out the foundation of the whole of philosophy, then you must derive feeling and the faculty of desire, as a single species, from the faculty of knowledge. Kant does not even claim to order those three faculties of the human being under one higher principle but allows them instead to remain merely coordinated.
>
> I agree with you completely that they can be subordinated to a higher principle but disagree that this principle can be that of the theoretical faculty. On this latter point I am in agreement with Kant, but I disagree with his view that those three faculties are not to be subordinated at all [to anything higher]. *I subordinate them to the principle of subjectivity in general.*[51]

Fichte's statement here that the starting point of the *Wissenschaftslehre* is a "principle of subjectivity in general" is consistent with our account of his development after 1794 and, more specifically, with our conclusion that subsequent to the WL 1794 Fichte came to believe that the content of his first principle must somehow embrace both the theoretical and practical aspects of the I.

51. "Ich subordiniere sie dem Prinzip der Subjektivität überhaupt" (my emphasis, GA, III.2, pp. 314–15).

Moreover, this passage lends support to our suggestion that the unity of theoretical and practical reason in the deepest sense – as opposed to a mere juxtaposition, or "coordination," of the two – is to be located in the fact that both are capable of being subsumed under a single, more general principle. This same theme becomes even more prominent in Fichte's texts of 1797–9. In his "First Introduction to the *Wissenschaftslehre*," for example, Fichte describes his starting point, the notion of the self-positing subject, as a characterization of the *single* activity of the I, which constitutes the "one essential nature of consciousness."[52] In his *Foundation of Natural Right* of 1796 Fichte says even more explicitly that the notion of self-positing is intended to "comprehend both practical and theoretical activity at once as [the I's] activity in general (*überhaupt*)."[53]

What these passages do not explain, however, is precisely how such a "principle of subjectivity in general" is to be understood. Although Fichte never really provides a more explicit elaboration, I shall suggest that his position is best understood in the following way: The demand that the accounts of both theoretical and practical reason begin from a common principle and be carried out within a unitary system is based upon the implicit belief that a single principle exists that expresses the fundamental nature of subjectivity itself and in terms of which all of consciousness, theoretical as well as practical, can be comprehended. Another way of formulating this position is to say that a single, essential structure ("the one essential nature of consciousness") underlies and informs the whole of subjectivity and that it is the task of philosophy's first principle to articulate the nature of this fundamental structure.

In some sense, then, the first principle can be understood as a statement about the essential nature of "I-hood" (*Ichheit*), or of subjectivity *überhaupt*. Furthermore, it is in this general structure of subjectivity that the unity of reason in its deepest sense can be said to reside. This unity is no longer regarded as consisting merely in the fact that the principles of both theoretical and practical reason can be deduced within a single system as conditions

---

52. "Das Eine Wesen der Intelligenz." As noted previously, this first introduction was published in 1797 and belongs to the system of 1797–9 (SW, I, p. 441).
53. *Grundlage des Naturrechts nach Prinzipien der Wissenschaftslehre*, GA, I.3, pp. 313–460 and I.4, pp. 1–165; SW, III, pp. 1–385. The passage cited here occurs at SW, III, p. 27.

of the same fundamental feature of consciousness (i.e., its formal unity). Rather, theoretical and practical reason constitute a unity in the sense that each exhibits the same internal structure, that of subjectivity in general – or, what is the same for Fichte, the structure of reason itself.[54] What Kant was ultimately constrained to regard as two distinct species of reason will be shown by the *Wissenschaftslehre* to be merely two manifestations of a single rational faculty.

Furthermore, it is important to recall here that what is asserted by this principle is no longer regarded by Fichte as an indubitable or apodictic "fact" but as a hypothesis whose truth can be decided only on the basis of its success in founding a complete philosophical system. Thus, the ultimate verification of Fichte's initial assertion about the essence of subjectivity is gained only at the end of the philosophical process, after it has been shown to enable philosophy to comprehend the totality of experience. For this reason the task of evaluating Fichte's success in actually proving his starting point clearly exceeds the scope of the present project. It will not be possible to assess Fichte's claim to have established a complete system that includes a deduction of every feature of experience from the principle of causality to the feelings of pleasure and pain. In what follows we shall focus upon one aspect of this larger project: What sense is it possible to make of Fichte's position that both theoretical and practical reason can be accounted for in terms of a single essential structure? It should be obvious that in concentrating upon this question we shall address the issue of the unity of theoretical and practical reason more directly than Fichte's efforts to prove the reality of practical reason. Yet it would be a mistake to think of the former as completely irrelevant to the latter. For if it can be shown that the employment of practical reason requires a similarly structured subject as theoretical reason, that is, consists in the same "basic activity of the mind," then the belief in the practical capacity for self-determination, if not exactly proved, becomes at least a more plausible hypothesis.

In the next two chapters we shall examine Fichte's attempt to understand both theoretical and practical reason in terms of the single fundamental structure of subjectivity articulated in his sys-

54. The *System of the Doctrine of Morals* (1798) begins with the following claim: "Subjectivity (*die Ichheit*), intelligence, reason . . . is [the single] point . . . from which our system begins" (SW, IV, p. 1).

tem's first principle. Although he formulates numerous versions of this principle in the period between 1794 and 1799, it is quite clearly the notion of self-positing that is central to all of them. For this reason we shall need to examine the concept of self-positing in general by addressing two main points: first, Fichte's notion of the subject as *Tathandlung* and, second, his characterization of self-positing as "an activity that returns into itself."[55] In addition, we shall need to consider how this structure informs both theoretical and practical consciousness by showing how Fichte attempts to give an account of the basic phenomena of each (self-consciousness in the former case and self-determination in the latter) in terms of the subject's self-positing activity. Finally, we shall examine the notion of self-determination that results from this account of practical reason, comparing it with Kant's own conception and assessing the merits of the view to which Fichte is led.

55. "[Ein] in sich zurückkehrendes Handeln" (SW, I, p. 462). Fichte uses this and similar expressions in numerous passages: SW, I, pp. 458, 461, 522, 532.

3

THE SELF-POSITING SUBJECT
AND THEORETICAL
SELF-CONSCIOUSNESS

This chapter marks the beginning of our attempt to reconstruct in some detail the theory of subjectivity centered around Fichte's notion of the self-positing subject. In this respect our interpretation is based upon one of the few claims about Fichte with which everyone can agree, namely, that the concept most fundamental to his theory of subjectivity is that of the self-positing subject, or, alternatively, "the absolute I." Unfortunately, once we venture beyond this most general claim, consensus among interpreters of Fichte essentially ceases. This is evidenced not only by the lack of any generally accepted, comprehensive interpretation of Fichte's thought, but also by the fact that there is widespread disagreement over the most elementary aspects of his principal doctrines, including that of the self-positing subject. For this reason one of our main aims here is simply to articulate in as coherent a form as possible the content of the conception of the subject that Fichte came to espouse. This alone is a sufficiently formidable task, given the obscurity of the texts involved and the great divergence of opinion among expositors of Fichte at even this basic interpretive level. This expository aspect of our project will be guided by the hypothesis that Fichte's development of the theory of the absolute subject is best understood as an attempt to come to terms with some of the implications of Kant's theory of self-consciousness –

especially the doctrine of transcendental apperception – and to do so within an essentially Critical framework.[1] In other words, I shall take seriously Fichte's own understanding of his relationship to Kant, as he expresses it in the following claim made in 1797, four years after developing his notion of the self-positing subject: "I have always said, and I say it here again, that my system is none other than the Kantian. That is, it contains the same view of things, even though its method is completely independent of Kant's presentation."[2]

At the same time, our concern will be not merely to restate Fichte's views but to understand them as well. That is, we shall want to know, as far as is possible, why Fichte espoused the positions he did. To this end we shall attempt to develop an account of the various factors that led Fichte to the notion of the self-positing subject. In addition to a consideration of the philosophical arguments in support of his theory, it will be necessary to look at the immediate historical context within which that theory developed. This will require a consideration of not only Kant's views but also those of lesser known figures whose reception and interpretation of Kant played a crucial role in shaping Fichte's own approach to the issues he addressed.

The aspect of Fichte's theory with which we are concerned here has its beginnings in the *Wissenschaftslehre* of 1794 but is articulated most clearly and consistently in the system of 1797–9. In the preceding chapter I argued that in the system of 1797–9 the concept of the self-positing subject was meant to capture the essential nature of subjectivity in both its theoretical and practical forms. Yet we also saw, particularly in Part I of the WL 1794, that Fichte originally developed his conception of the subject in connection with a particular issue from the domain of theoretical philosophy, namely, theoretical self-consciousness. Hence, our first step in understanding Fichte's theory of subjectivity will be to examine his account of theoretical self-consciousness and to articulate the notion of the self-positing subject that emerges from that account.

This way of proceeding raises an important question concerning Fichte's overall project: In what sense does Fichte intend to claim that theoretical reason as a whole, and not merely one aspect

---

1. In this fundamental respect my interpretation is inspired by a doctoral dissertation written by Benson (1974), as well as by Pippin (1988, 1989).
2. SW, I, p. 420.

of it (i.e., self-consciousness), is grounded in the activity of self-positing? In the WL 1794 it is clear that Fichte envisioned a system in which the categories of the understanding and the forms of sensible intuition could be deduced by a dialectical chain of arguments that was generated by a basic contradiction between the principle of the self-positing I and the second principle of philosophy: "The I posits a not-I in opposition to itself." This claim is not examined in detail here, in part because there is some doubt about the extent of Fichte's commitment to this project in later versions of the *Wissenschaftslehre* (including the system of 1797–9), but also because it belongs to that class of German Idealism's ambitious aims that, although philosophically provocative, are almost certainly incapable of actually being carried out. Yet, even if we abstract from Fichte's claim to be able to deduce the principles of theoretical reason from his system's first two principles, it is still possible to understand the principle of self-positing as fundamental to the whole of theoretical reason in the following sense: The very possibility of theoretical subjectivity can be understood as dependent upon the subject's self-positing activity, since for Fichte (as well as for Kant), the self-consciousness at issue here constitutes the most basic condition upon which the possibility of all empirical knowledge depends.

In the present chapter, then, we shall focus rather narrowly on issues relevant only to theoretical self-consciousness, postponing until the next chapter a discussion of whatever implications Fichte's account might have for a theory of subjectivity in general. Our treatment of theoretical self-consciousness is divided into three sections, each of which focuses on one central aspect of the theory. In the first section we shall discuss the nature of the distinctive self-awareness that Fichte attributes to the "self-positing" subject, an awareness that he sometimes characterizes as "intellectual intuition." In the second part we shall examine the arguments that allegedly support Fichte's view, especially the claim that his account of self-awareness has a transcendental grounding. Finally, we shall look at Fichte's discussion of the peculiar sense in which the subject of consciousness can be said to "exist."

Self-positing as nonrepresentational
self-awareness

This first section examines Fichte's views concerning the unique, nonrepresentational nature of self-awareness. In its most general form Fichte's claim will be that the subject is at all times present to itself within consciousness but that its mode of being present to itself is fundamentally distinct from the way in which it is conscious of objects. Our task will be to understand precisely how the subject's awareness of itself differs from the consciousness of objects. In light of the widespread disagreement surrounding the notion of the self-positing subject, we shall first approach Fichte's theory via an indirect route, beginning with an examination of the nature of the problem that the theory was originally intended to solve. Following this path, our first question becomes: What constitutes "Fichte's problem"? In what has become one of the most influential of recent interpretations, Dieter Henrich takes Fichte's central problem to consist in a number of related paradoxes that allegedly arise when one attempts to explain the possibility of self-consciousness.[3] Although it cannot be denied that Fichte's project is closely bound up with the task of finding an adequate account of self-consciousness, Henrich's exclusive concern with this issue ultimately has the effect of distorting the central issue in a fundamental way. For Fichte's problem arises not out of a consideration of the phenomenon of *self*-consciousness per se, but in the wider context of a theory of consciousness in general. Moreover, it is only by locating Fichte's concern within this wider framework that his problem, as he himself understood it, becomes visible. This "wider context," of course, is Kant's theory of consciousness or, more accurately, Kant's theory as it was understood by his immediate successors. Although both of the passages in which Fichte explicitly lays out what I take to be his central problem date from 1797, three years after the first published version of the *Wissenschaftslehre*, clues to the origins of this problem, as well as an account of the context in which it emerges, are to be found in an early text of 1794, the *Aenesidemus* review.[4] Since our present aim is to understand the precise nature of this issue, it will be helpful to begin with a brief consideration of the relevant passages of this review.

The *Aenesidemus* review constitutes Fichte's first serious endeavor to come to terms with some of the problems faced by contemporary

3. This interpretation is found in Henrich (1982). In German as "Fichtes ursprüngliche Einsicht" (1966, pp. 188–232). Earlier versions of this article appear as "Fichte's 'Ich' " in Henrich (1982, pp. 57–82) and as "La découverte de Fichte" (1967, pp. 154–69). For a short account and criticism of Henrich's interpretation, see Pippin (1988, pp. 80–4).

4. GA, 1.2, pp. 41–67; SW, I, pp. 3–25.

followers of Kant who attempted to reconstruct and defend Kant's system. The review itself represents Fichte's response to some of the skeptical objections leveled against Critical Philosophy by G. E. Schulze in his book *Aenesidemus*.[5] Our efforts to understand Fichte's defense of Kant against Schulze are complicated by the historical fact that Schulze's book itself was a response to a particular version of Critical Philosophy, namely that of Reinhold. In his reconstruction of Kant's system, Reinhold's intention was not to criticize Kant's basic positions but rather to purify them of their inconsistencies and to recast them in a more systematic form. Without entering into all of the details of Reinhold's notion of a philosophical system, it suffices for our present purposes to note that part of Reinhold's attempt to systematize Critical Philosophy involved a search for the "highest" principle of philosophy, a principle from which all other philosophical truths could be derived.[6] Since Reinhold understood Kant's philosophy as primarily a philosophy of consciousness, his first principle was at the same time a characterization of the most general concept needed to give an account of all of the contents of consciousness. This most general concept for Reinhold was that of *Vorstellung,* or "representation," and was expressed in what Reinhold termed the "principle of consciousness" (*der Satz des Bewußtseins*): "In consciousness the subject distinguishes the representation from the subject and the object and relates it to both."[7]

Reinhold's principle can be understood as making two general philosophical claims: The first is that *all* conscious states, whether cognitive, volitional, or affective, share a single underlying structure. Although this claim does not appear explicitly in Reinhold's formulation of the principle itself, it follows from his conception of its role as the first principle of a comprehensive philosophy of consciousness. The second claim spells out what this basic structure of consciousness is, identifying it with the structure that Reinhold ascribes to *Vorstellung.* On this view, all consciousness involves not

---

5. Schulze ([1792], 1911).
6. Although Fichte initially stood under the spell of Reinhold's conception of a philosophical system (especially in *Ueber den Begriff der Wissenschaftslehre* but also in the WL 1794), his writings after this point are considerably less informed by the notion of system in Reinhold's sense. My approach in this chapter will be to deemphasize Fichte's early views on method in favor of what I consider to be his philosophically more interesting theory of the subject.
7. "Im Bewußtsein wird die Vorstellung durch das Subjekt vom Subjekt und Objekt unterschieden und auf beide bezogen" (Reinhold, 1790, p. 167).

only a subject that is distinct from its object, but a third element as well – a *representation*, which the subject distinguishes both from itself and from the object. In other words, the subject of consciousness not only distinguishes itself from its representation; it also makes a distinction between the representation and the object which that representation is a representation of. In addition to these two species of "distinguishing," consciousness also involves two kinds of "relating," since the subject relates the representation both to itself and to the object. It is the first of these – the subject's relation to its representations – that will be of most concern to Fichte, and for this reason we shall consider the nature of this "relating" in greater detail later.

Fichte's primary criticism of Reinhold in the *Aenesidemus* review consists in the claim that representation, or *Vorstellung*, is unable to serve as the highest, most general concept for a philosophy that intends to use such a concept as the basis for an understanding of consciousness in its entirety. Although Fichte's text itself provides few clues to the reasoning behind his rejection of Reinhold's basic claim, a look at Schulze's own objections to Reinhold's principle helps to supply the missing argument. As we saw earlier, Reinhold's principle asserts that all consciousness involves a dual relationship – a "relating" and a "distinguishing" – between representation and subject. On the one hand, the representation is *distinguished* from the subject. Thus, I recognize my representation of an object as distinct from myself, the representing subject. On the other hand, every representation is *related* to a subject in the sense that all of my representations are regarded as belonging to a particular subject, namely, to me. Schulze's point is that if all consciousness involves this relation between representation and subject, and if this relating occurs "within" consciousness as Reinhold's principle claims, then consciousness must also involve some kind of awareness of that subject. In other words, in order to relate a representation to myself as subject, in order to recognize it as mine, I must in some sense be aware of myself as subject. But this self-awareness on the part of the subject cannot itself be accounted for in terms of the structure that Reinhold attributes to representation. The reason for this is easily grasped: If the self-awareness involved in my representation of X were itself a species of representation, then there would need to be another subject distinguished from and related to that representation of myself, and so on ad infinitum. An account of even the simplest state of consciousness would require the assumption of an infinite number of subjects and an infinite number of acts of relating between subject and representation.

Whereas Schulze's conclusion that the self-consciousness involved in representational consciousness cannot itself be another species of representation is regarded by him as a decisive critique of the Critical theory of consciousness in general, for Fichte it takes on a different meaning. For him, Schulze's criticism implies that the defender of Critical Philosophy must reject Reinhold's claim that the structure of representational consciousness is the structure of *all* consciousness and must provide instead an account of the self-awareness involved in representational consciousness that avoids the infinite regress into which any account based on Reinhold's model inevitably falls. Thus, it should come as no surprise that this task – a characterization of self-awareness in nonrepresentational terms – should appear to Fichte as the principal challenge for anyone wishing to defend the basic soundness of Critical Philosophy.[8]

Before turning to Fichte's response to Schulze in the *Aenesidemus* review, it is worth calling attention to two points about this account of Fichte's problem. The first concerns the great irony that surrounds the philosophical exchange just depicted. For it is Schulze, the skeptic and critic of Kant, who, in criticizing Reinhold, the most prominent Kantian of his time, forces Fichte to rediscover what, at least in a very general sense, is a truly Kantian position – namely, that self-awareness, as it is treated by Kant under the title "pure apperception," is to be understood in terms fundamentally different from those that apply to the consciousness of objects. Although this "rediscovery" of Kant's position coheres nicely with Fichte's frequent claims to being the only true Kantian among his contemporaries, it does not, of course, exhaust the issue of Fichte's relationship to Kant. For, as we shall see later, the theory of the self-positing subject is not *merely* a rediscovery of Kant's own position on the topic of self-consciousness. In order to settle the issue of Fichte's relationship to his predecessor, we shall need eventually to ask as well whether those aspects of Fichte's theory

8. Thus, Fichte's task exhibits striking similarities to Sartre's account of consciousness, which is constructed around a fundamental distinction between intentional, or thetic, consciousness of an object and nonintentional, nonthetic self-consciousness. The similarities between these two positions will become even more apparent later. See Sartre (1966, pp. 9–17; 1957, pp. 31–54).

that go beyond Kant's explicit position on this score are consistent with, or in violation of, the spirit of Critical Philosophy.

Second, we are now in a position to see that the problem of self-awareness addressed by Fichte in the *Aenesidemus* review is identical to the one articulated by him in two separate passages from 1797. Consider the following passage from the "Attempt at a New Presentation of the *Wissenschaftslehre*," in which Fichte lays out the problem that is supposed to provide the principal motivation behind his theory of the self-positing subject:

> Insofar as you are conscious of some object – for example, the wall in front of you – you are . . . conscious of your thinking (*deines Denkens*) of this wall, and a consciousness of the wall is possible only insofar as you are conscious of your thinking. But in order to be conscious of your thinking, you must be conscious of yourself. . . . [Thus,] no object comes to consciousness except under the condition that I am also conscious of myself, the conscious subject. This principle is incontrovertible. But if it is claimed that in this self-consciousness I am an object to myself, then what was true of the subject in the previous case [i.e., in the consciousness of the wall] must also hold for the subject here [i.e., in self-consciousness]. It too becomes an object and requires a new subject, and so on ad infinitum. On this view, subject and object are distinct from each other in every state of consciousness, and . . . this is the reason why . . . consciousness cannot be accounted for in this manner.[9]

Although Fichte's problem *is* concerned with self-awareness and with the task of understanding it in a way that avoids an infinite regress, it is important to see that Fichte arrives at this problem not simply by way of an inquiry into the phenomenon of self-consciousness per se but rather along a path that starts from a theory of consciousness in general and leads to the problem of characterizing the nature of the self-awareness that is involved *in every*

9. SW, I, pp. 526–7. The second passage is found at GA, IV.2, p. 30. It is the latter which Henrich (1982) cites (p. 22) in support of his own interpretation, but in doing so he omits the passage's first sentence, which actually serves as a crucial premise for the paradox Fichte lays out: "We cannot be aware of external objects without being aware of ourselves, that is, without being an object for ourselves." Note that Fichte's conclusion (in both passages) is that *consciousness* (not self-consciousness) "cannot be accounted for in this manner." Thus, the problem to which Fichte is pointing is not, strictly speaking, a problem of self-consciousness per se but one that arises within a larger theory of consciousness in general.

representational state. Thus, as Fichte himself makes quite explicit, the problem to which he is calling our attention depends upon the specific assumption, inherited from Reinhold's account of representation, that all consciousness of objects requires a kind of self-awareness. The problem arises when one realizes, as Schulze pointed out, that this self-awareness cannot itself have the structure that Reinhold attributed to representational consciousness. Given this account of the genesis of Fichte's view, one might ask whether, in accepting Reinhold's description of representational consciousness, especially its insistence that *each* representation is related within consciousness to a subject, Fichte does not already subscribe to a position that Kant himself would reject. For, as is well known, Kant held not that the "I think" does in fact accompany each of my representations, but only that it must be able to do so. This is indeed an important question, but since our present concern is primarily to articulate the content of Fichte's understanding of the nature of self-awareness, we shall postpone a consideration of this problem for now and return to it in the second section of this chapter.

Once we understand the nature of the problem pointed out by Schulze, the path which Fichte must take to solve it becomes clearer: In order to save what he takes to be the Critical doctrine that every representation of an object is related within consciousness to the subject of consciousness, he must find a way to characterize this relation that does not rely upon the structure of representational consciousness, in which the subject of awareness is always distinct from what it represents. This is indeed the position that Fichte begins to stake out in a passage from the *Aenesidemus* review that anticipates, in both language and substance, his more developed theory of the self-positing subject:

> The absolute subject, the I, is not given through empirical intuition but is posited (*gesetzt*) through intellectual intuition. . . . [It is] not present within empirical consciousness except insofar as a representation is related to [it]. . . . One can never become conscious of the absolute subject – that which represents but is not represented – . . . as something empirically given.[10]

Although this passage does not shed much light on the nuts and bolts of the theory that Fichte will ultimately develop, it is of

10. SW, I, p. 10.

considerable importance to our attempt to understand the notion of the self-positing subject, for, as an argument directed explicitly at Schulze's critique of Reinhold, it points out the intimate connection between the problem of an infinite regress raised by Schulze and Fichte's theory of the self-positing subject. More specifically, it makes clear that Fichte coins the term 'positing' as a direct response to Schulze and that he does so in order to distinguish the subject's nonrepresentational awareness of itself from "empirical" (i.e., objective, or representational) consciousness. Moreover, Fichte's statement that "the I is not present within empirical consciousness except insofar as a representation is related to it" suggests what kind of self-awareness Fichte intends to designate by the term 'positing', namely, the subject's "relation" to each of its representations, which, as we know from our analysis of Reinhold's principle of consciousness, refers to the subject's awareness of its representations as belonging to itself.

Apart from the use of the term 'positing' in connection with "intellectual intuition" (a topic to which we return later), there are very few clues in this early passage to help us determine more precisely the nature of the awareness that is at issue. We can do somewhat better by looking at Fichte's account four years later of the general strategy required to solve his problem of the nature of self-awareness. In this later passage Fichte makes clear that the infinite regress arises only if one understands self-awareness as "a state of the mind or [as] an object." Consequently, the problem "can be resolved only by discovering something in which consciousness is simultaneously both object and subject, that is, by exhibiting *an immediate consciousness*."[11] The logic of the strategy behind Fichte's response to Schulze is clear: In order to avoid an infinite regress in a general account of representational consciousness, the self-awareness required for that consciousness may not itself be representational (i.e., marked by a distinction between the subject and object of awareness) but must instead be "immediate" consciousness. Although, at a general level, this strategy is clear enough, Fichte's theory of self-positing must be able to give a more precise characterization of the nature of this "immediate" consciousness.

It seems natural to begin this task with the assumption that the kind of awareness involved in the doctrine of self-positing is to be

11. GA, IV.2, p. 30.

equated with self-consciousness. This seems to follow both from our discussion of the historical background of Fichte's problem and from Fichte's own references to self-positing as a kind of self-consciousness. Yet Fichte often emphasizes that intellectual intuition, or self-positing, is *distinct* from self-consciousness: "[Self-positing] is a pure *intuition*. Thus, it is not a consciousness, not even a self-consciousness."[12] The characterization of self-positing as an intuition but not as "a consciousness" seems paradoxical at first glance, but Fichte explains this distinction in the following passage:

> In ordinary consciousness . . . pure self-consciousness [i.e., the awareness involved in self-positing] does not constitute a complete state of consciousness. Rather, it is only a necessary component by means of which consciousness first becomes possible. . . . Neither self-consciousness nor sensible intuition nor a concept is by itself a representation. Rather, they are those elements by means of which representations become possible. According to Kant . . . and to me, three elements go to make up a complete representation: 1) that by means of which the representation is related to an object and becomes the representation of *something*, which we agree in calling sensible intuition; . . . 2) that by means of which the representation is related to the subject and becomes *my* representation. (Although Kant . . . does not call this element an intuition, I do because it stands in the same relation to a complete representation as does sensible intuition.) And, finally, 3) that which unifies both . . . and which we again agree in calling a concept.[13]

The first thing to be noticed here is that although self-positing *is* characterized as a kind of self-consciousness, it is qualified by the adjective 'pure' (in other instances Fichte uses the term 'immediate'). Moreover, this passage helps to make clear part of what it means for Fichte to call self-positing "pure" or "immediate" self-consciousness. The awareness involved in self-positing is a kind of *self*-awareness that, though a necessary component (*Bestandteil*) of every conscious state, never constitutes by itself a complete state of consciousness. The reason that pure self-consciousness cannot stand alone becomes clearer when we determine more precisely the content of this self-awareness.

In later texts Fichte commonly characterizes self-positing as an immediate intuition of the activity of thought.[14] This characterization is reminiscent of the claim, cited earlier, that my conscious-

12. SW, I, p. 459.   13. SW, I, pp. 473–4.   14. SW, I, p. 522.

ness of an object always involves an awareness of my thinking (*meines Denkens*). This suggests that at least part of the doctrine of the self-positing subject involves the claim that the activity of thought always includes an awareness of itself *as* thinking – or that consciousness is necessarily aware of itself *as* consciousness. According to this view, then, all consciousness of objects requires an activity of thought that is directed at an object and, at the same time, "*self*-positing" in the sense that it always carries with it an awareness of itself as engaged in the activity of thinking. Hence, the consciousness of an object always involves a kind of self-awareness on the part of the subject of consciousness. The I that is conscious is at the same time immediately aware that it is conscious.[15] Thus, it is understandable that Fichte also describes this self-awareness as an immediate awareness of my having the particular representations I do: "When I say that I represent something, this is equivalent to saying the following: 'I am aware that I have a representation of this object.' "[16] Moreover, this characterization of self-positing is consistent with Fichte's assertion, quoted earlier, that it is through self-positing that the representation becomes related to the subject.

At this point we are in a position to understand why Fichte characterizes self-positing as pure and spontaneous, and why he regards it, in what seems to be an outright violation of orthodox Kantianism, as a species of intellectual intuition. In the first place, 'intellectual intuition' is often used to denote a kind of cognition in which the subject's intuiting activity is, in some sense, indistinguishable from the object of intuition. One historically significant version of this conception is the notion of a divine intuition that, in knowing its objects, *creates* them. Of course, Fichte's doctrine of intellectual intuition should not be understood as attributing to the human intellect the power of creating its objects of knowledge; what it borrows from this theological conception, rather, is the general notion of a species of awareness in which the distinction that is normally made between the intuiter and that which is intuited does not apply, a state of affairs that Fichte wants to ascribe, in some form, to the subject's self-positing.[17] (Actually, Fichte's notion of intellectual intuition is somewhat closer to the

15. GA, IV.2, p. 30.
16. SW, I, p. 473. Although here Fichte is quoting a passage from J. F. Schulz, it is clear that he agrees with Schulz on this point.
17. See, e.g., GA, II.3, p. 144: "that which is intuited is at the same time the intuition."

notion of a creative intellect than the present disclaimer implies. For, although the Fichtean intellect does not create its *objects,* there is an important sense in which the activity of intellectual intuition does constitute the subject of thought. We return to this difficult but crucial aspect of Fichte's doctrine in the section on self-positing as self-constituting existence.)

Beyond this consideration, however, there is a more specific reason, one more intimately connected to Kant's own position, for choosing the term 'intellectual intuition'. By now it should be clear that much of Fichte's doctrine can be understood in the context of Kant's views regarding the "I think" that must be able to accompany all of my representations. And, when viewed in this light, the characterization of self-positing as a kind of intellectual intuition no longer appears as blatantly un-Kantian as it seems at first sight. Rather, it can be regarded as one natural way of dealing with the difficulties encountered by Kant in trying to say what kind of awareness is involved in the "I think." For Kant, the recognition that a particular representation X belongs to me is to be distinguished conceptually from a simple, un-self-conscious awareness of X. Unlike the latter, the awareness of myself as having particular representations is not itself an empirical state of affairs and is therefore not given through sensible intuition but is to be attributed rather to the subject's spontaneity. At the same time, the "I think" possesses for Kant a specific characteristic that suggests that it be understood as a species of *intuition.* For the "I think" involves more than merely the thought, or concept, of a subject; it also provides an immediate awareness of the subject's *existence* – something that, for Kant, only intuition is capable of giving.[18] As Fichte points out, Kant denies that there is a human faculty of intellectual intuition because he understands such a faculty to be the capacity for an immediate acquaintance with things in themselves. Here, of course, Fichte is in complete agreement with Kant. His point, rather, is that Kant's dichotomy of concept and sensible intuition is insufficient to characterize the subject's immediate awareness of its own conscious activity, and that the features of this awareness naturally lead one to understand it as a kind of intellectual intuition.

It should now also be clear why Fichte makes the claim that self-positing as such cannot alone constitute a state of consciousness.

---

18. A consideration of the sense in which the subject "exists" in intellectual intuition will be postponed until the final section of this chapter.

If intellectual intuition consists in the awareness of my having the representations I do, then in order for it to occur, there must be representations present to consciousness to be recognized as my own.[19] These representations, however, can be given only through sensible intuition. Thus, an awareness of my conscious activity is possible only on the condition that that activity also be directed at an object other than itself. For this reason, Fichte claims that intellectual intuition is always conjoined with sensible intuition. This view might also be expressed as the thesis that consciousness as a whole is informed by a dual structure.[20] On the one hand, consciousness is always directed at an empirical object supplied through sensible intuition. On the other hand, consciousness is essentially self-referential in that each representation also necessarily enters into a relationship to one and the same subject. It is this self-referential aspect of consciousness that is expressed in the claim that the subject is "*self*-positing."

Fichte explicitly sets out the thesis of the dual structure of consciousness in the following passage:

> Consciousness, as such, *observes itself* (*sieht sich selbst zu*). This self-observation is immediately united with everything that belongs to consciousness, and the nature of consciousness consists in this *immediate* unity of being and seeing. . . . Thus, in consciousness there is, figuratively speaking, a double series of being and observing, of the real and the ideal, and its essence consists in the inseparability of these two elements.[21]

The "dual series" to which Fichte refers is to be understood in terms of the claim that every consciousness of an object X involves two conceptually distinct components that are inseparable within

19. The distinction employed here between intellectual and sensible intuition should not be taken to imply that Fichte simply takes over, unmodified, Kant's dichotomy between the subject's spontaneous activity and a purely receptive faculty of sensible intuition. Fichte clearly makes a distinction between intellectual and sensible intuition (e.g., SW, I, p. 464), although, of course, *ultimately* he (as well as Hegel after him) will want to reject this dichotomy in the sense that he will try to understand even the content of empirical intuition as grounded, at least to some extent, in the subject's activity. This point has been touched upon in the earlier discussion of Fichte's notion of the *Anstoß*, although it remains, in the thought of both Fichte and Hegel, a very obscure doctrine.

20. Once again, the deep affinity between the views of Sartre and Fichte becomes apparent, for Sartre also puts such a dual structure at the center of his theory of consciousness.

21. SW, I, pp. 435–6.

actual consciousness: an outward, object-directed awareness (a consciousness of X) and an inward, self-referential awareness (a consciousness that I am conscious of X).[22] Of course, Fichte's characterization of the latter component as a kind of "self-observation" is, as he himself points out, merely figurative. In the first place, the term 'observation' is borrowed from discourse about objective consciousness and implies the very distinction between observer and observed that Fichte wants to claim is irrelevant in the case of self-positing. Second, as we have already seen, the self-positing subject does not really observe "itself," at least not in the sense that it attains a "picture" of itself, as if regarding its image in a mirror. The conscious subject never succeeds in making itself into its own object. Its "self-observation," rather, refers merely to consciousness's awareness of its states, that is, to its awareness that it is aware.

Certainly the most difficult aspect of Fichte's notion of the dual structure of consciousness is the idea that each state of consciousness is composed of two elements, each of which is itself a kind of awareness. Although Fichte provides very little to aid our understanding of the relation between these two components, we can begin with his characterization of their unity as "immediate" and "inseparable." That the two components are inseparable undoubtedly refers to the fact that neither can occur within consciousness without the other – a sensible intuition without intellectual intuition could not be recognized as part of *my* consciousness, and, conversely, in order for intellectual intuition to occur, there must be an empirical intuition to be appropriated as "mine." What it means to attribute *immediate* unity to the two mental acts involved in a representational state is, however, less clear. Nevertheless, we can find a clue to part of Fichte's meaning in a later passage from the same text: "The philosopher does not immediately find this intellectual intuition . . . as an isolated fact of consciousness but discovers it rather by distinguishing among what, within ordinary consciousness, occurs as unified, and by breaking the whole into its component parts."[23] Hence, the immediate unity of self-positing and sensible intuition refers to the fact that ordinary consciousness, in contrast to a *philosophical* understanding of consciousness, is not itself aware of its dual structure; that is, it is not directly aware of the fact that there are two distinguishable acts of awareness that comprise each single state of consciousness.

22. This point is nicely made by Benson (1974, p. 188).   23. SW, I, p. 465.

The most important implication of the thesis of the "immediate unity" of intellectual and empirical intuition is that the two mental acts that constitute a single conscious state are not to be understood as two separate but simultaneous states that somehow overlap. It is certainly not Fichte's intention to claim, for example, that in every instance of ordinary visual perception there are two fully constituted conscious states corresponding to the judgments "I see X" and "I know that I am seeing X." The implausibility of an account of consciousness that would require an explicit, second-order consciousness of the "I think" to accompany all representations suggests that the kind of awareness Fichte ascribes to intellectual intuition must be understood as implicit in nature. On this view, the "immediate" self-awareness of intellectual intuition would have to be understood as prereflective and unarticulated in any explicit sense. This merely implicit self-awareness would then stand in contrast to what I shall call "reflective self-consciousness," which is to be understood as a full-fledged state of consciousness resulting from the subject consciously directing its attention to itself and making its own subjectivity its object.[24] The distinction referred to earlier between self-positing and self-consciousness suggests this distinction between the implicit, immediate self-awareness of intellectual intuition and an explicit, fully articulated self-conscious state.

There are numerous passages in Fichte's texts that directly contrast the act of self-positing with what the conscious subject does when it deliberately reflects upon itself. One such passage from the *Wissenschaftslehre nova methodo* confirms that Fichte did in fact conceive of the difference between these two acts in terms of the distinction between immediate and reflective self-consciousness that I have suggested here:

> Let everyone now think of his I and pay attention to how he does this. Now, in contrast, let everyone think of an external object. In this latter case we do not notice (*bemerken*) ourselves as the thinker of the object. That is, we do not notice that we are the thinker of the object but rather disappear, so to speak, in the object. Nevertheless,

---

24. The term 'reflective self-consciousness' is inspired by Sartre, who, like Fichte, distinguishes "nonthetic" self-consciousness, which is involuntary and universally present, from reflective self-consciousness, which is optional and consists in reflecting upon oneself as an object, for example, of possible knowledge.

it is easily and obviously discovered that the thinker and that which is thought are distinct from each other.[25]

Fichte's initial challenge to "think one's I" is obviously a call to engage in reflection, to bring about a state of explicit, reflective self-consciousness. This consciously undertaken reflection must be understood as distinct from the activity of self-positing, which is part of all conscious states and occurs independently of the subject's volition. What is most important here is Fichte's assertion that in the consciousness of an object the subject does not explicitly "notice" itself as the thinker of its thoughts but "disappears" into the object. Unless we are to give up Fichte's fundamental claim that an act of intellectual intuition is involved in every conscious state (a claim discussed more fully in the following section), we must take his assertion that the subject disappears in objective consciousness to mean that the subject, in directing its attention to an external object, has no *explicit* consciousness of itself. That there is, however, an implicit self-awareness in objective consciousness is suggested by the next statement that the difference between the thinker and its thought is "easily and obviously discovered." Part of the "immediate" nature of the self-awareness of intellectual intuition seems, then, to consist in the fact that, although it is not explicitly present whenever I think an object, I have easy and immediate access to myself (or, more accurately, to the fact that my conscious state is mine) whenever I choose to make that state of affairs the object of my attention.[26]

Although Fichte's view does seem to include the claim that the awareness involved in self-positing is implicit, whereas that of reflective self-consciousness is of an explicit nature, it is also clear that this cannot be the only respect in which the two species of self-awareness differ. Reflective self-consciousness cannot be understood simply as an explicit awareness of the same content that is present, though only implicitly, in the subject's immediate self-awareness. For if the distinction between the two forms of self-consciousness is to halt the infinite regress that constituted

---

25. GA, IV.2, p. 29. Other passages with similar implications are pointed out by Pippin (1988, p. 82, n. 24).
26. See also Fichte's discussion of the "immediate" nature of self-positing at SW, I, p. 527: "The consciousness of my thinking is not something accidental to my thinking; it is not merely added on or attached to it; rather, it is inseparable from my thinking."

Fichte's initial problem, then they must also differ in *structure* and not merely in degree of awareness. This point is simply an implication of Fichte's basic claim that the subject's self-positing, in contrast to reflective self-consciousness, may not exhibit the structure of representational consciousness.

This realization leads us to an issue that lies at the heart of any theory that postulates a kind of prereflective self-awareness: What exactly is it that such nonrepresentational awareness is an awareness of, and how does the content of that awareness differ from that of reflective self-consciousness? As we have seen, to claim that self-positing is nonrepresentational in nature is to deny that the subject is constituted as an *object* for itself in its immediate self-awareness. But what, more precisely, does this mean? Although Fichte does not provide us with a fully elaborated answer to this question, we can get some idea of his position by piecing together a number of remarks made at different places throughout his discussion of the subject's self-positing, particularly in those passages where he contrasts sensible and intellectual intuition. The distinguishing feature of the former is that it has as its object "Being" (*ein Sein*), while the latter is directed, not at things, but at an *activity* or, as Fichte says, an "acting" (*ein Handeln*).[27] As we have seen, the "acting" that is at issue here is simply the activity of thinking, where the term 'thinking' (*das Denken*) is used broadly to designate something like representing, or conscious activity in general. The content of this awareness is further characterized by Fichte as "the immediate consciousness that I am acting and [of] what I am enacting. It is that by means of which I know something because I do it."[28] Thus, the subject's self-positing is to be understood as analogous to the kind of immediate awareness that an agent has of its own acting, including both the fact *that* it is acting, as well as the content of its deed. Presumably what is important to Fichte about this analogy is the notion that the awareness referred to is *internal* to, and therefore inseparable from, the agent's acting, an awareness without which the activity would no longer be an "acting." Thus, it is actually somewhat misleading to say, as Fichte does, that intellectual intuition is "directed at" the activity of consciousness. As his explication of that claim makes clear, what he means to assert is that the former is internal

27. SW, I, pp. 471–2. See also pp. 522, 527 and GA, IV.2, p. 30.
28. SW, I, p. 463.

to the latter – that part of what it is to think is to be aware of one-self as thinking. In other words, the nature of consciousness is such that there is no representing of X without a concurrent awareness that one is doing so.

A second aspect of what it means to deny that the subject is constituted as an object for itself in intellectual intuition can be formulated in the claim that such awareness is *nondiscursive* in nature. This implies that the subject's immediate positing of its representations as its own is not to be understood as involving a synthesis of diverse, otherwise unconnected units which are given independently of the activity that brings them together. Self-positing is not to be thought of as a composite of two distinguish-able elements, concept and intuition, but as a simple, unitary awareness. One way of spelling out this difference might be to distinguish between a still unarticulated awareness of one's repre-senting activity in general and a consciousness of self that is con-stituted through a synthesis of past instances of self-awareness. Immediate self-awareness, then, might be characterized as con-sciousness's ever-present awareness *that* it is conscious (and con-scious of a particular content). Reflective self-consciousness, however, would consist in the awareness of a particular represen-tation as *mine*, or as belonging to *me*, where the "I" to which my representations were ascribed would be a subject that was also recognized as identical with the subject of other, previous con-scious states. On this view, reflective self-consciousness would require, in addition to a fleeting, unsynthesized awareness *now* of my activity of thought, an explicit awareness of the numerical identity of the subject with respect to its past representational states.

Yet this way of distinguishing the two types of self-consciousness is not completely satisfactory, for it implies a conception of imme-diate self-awareness as subjectless, or as consisting merely in the awareness that *there is* a thinking taking place. But this, I believe, would be to misconstrue Fichte's view, for he seems to be claiming that intellectual intuition already includes some kind of awareness of the *I*. In other words, in my immediate self-awareness I am not aware merely that there is a representing going on presently; I am presumably also aware of this activity of consciousness as in some sense *my own*.[29] In contrast, then, to some later accounts of prere-

---

29. Although Fichte never explicitly distinguishes between these two alterna-tives, there is ample evidence that he takes the latter view. Recall first that

flective self-awareness,[30] Fichte seems to hold that, although the I first becomes fully constituted as an *object* in reflective self-consciousness, it does not first appear therein. Rather, already in intellectual intuition the I is present to itself in some form – not, of course, as a particular, individual self, but simply "as a subject," as a "conscious something" (*das Bewußtseiende*).[31]

Of course, it is notoriously difficult to specify what such a non-discursive, prereflective reference to an I would consist in. At the very least it would seem to require some awareness of the activity of representing that at the same time involved an apprehension of the unity, or identity, of the representing subject.[32] The difficulty here arises in specifying what that apprehension of the I's unity would consist in, if not in the awareness of some relation among its present and past representations. Yet this possibility seems to be ruled out by the requirement that self-positing be a simple awareness, one not constituted through a synthesis of past representational states. Even if this were not ruled out, however, how would the content of immediate self-awareness differ from that of reflective self-consciousness? Is intellectual intuition perhaps to be understood as a synthesizing intuition that actively *establishes* the subject's identity – unites its representations into a single consciousness – while reflective self-consciousness is merely an explicit awareness of this already constituted unity? And if so, is there a way of picturing the former activity? Is it, as it were, a fitting of each representation with some quality or marker that then makes it possible for them to be recognized as constituting a *single* consciousness? These are difficult questions that a fully elaborated Fichtean theory would have to address; for now perhaps it is sufficient simply to have made explicit the various properties that Fichte believes must be attributed to the subject's intellectual intuition. Thus, self-positing involves (1) an immediate, *nondiscursive*

already in Reinhold's formulation of the principle of consciousness each representation is said to be related to a *subject*. Moreover, Fichte consistently characterizes intellectual intuition not as awareness of *some* (anyone's) activity of thought, but (e.g., at SW, I, p. 526) as the awareness of *your* thought (*deines Denkens*).

30. The best known example of such a theory is Sartre's, especially in *The Transcendence of the Ego*.
31. GA, IV.2, p. 33.
32. For example, in WL 1794 Fichte explicates the notion of self-positing by means of the formula "I = I," which is said to express the fact that the I "is identical to (*gleich*) itself, always one and the same" (SW, I, p. 94).

awareness that consists in (2) the relating of the representations of consciousness to a *subject*, a relating that is (3) *internal* to and inseparable from the activity of consciousness itself.

Self-positing as a transcendental condition
of consciousness

If we accept the foregoing account as an accurate description of Fichte's view of the nature of self-awareness, we are still left with the question as to what reasons there might be for espousing such a view, a question that Fichte himself formulates in the following way: "If it must be conceded that there is no immediate, isolated consciousness of intellectual intuition, how then does the philosopher arrive at an isolated conception and knowledge of it?"[33] In other words, what grounds are there for believing that consciousness includes as one of its components an omnipresent but merely implicit self-awareness? In the same passage Fichte provides us with a partial answer: "Undoubtedly in the same way that he [i.e., the philosopher] arrives at an isolated conception and knowledge of sensible intuition, through inference from the obvious facts of consciousness." The assertion that our knowledge of self-positing is gained through an inference (*durch einen Schluß*) rather than through simple introspection reinforces the point alluded to earlier that the thesis of self-positing is not to be understood as a mere description of the facts of consciousness but rather as an account of the subject that is supported by more theoretical considerations. Indeed, this follows necessarily if we take seriously Fichte's frequently repeated claim that the act of self-positing is never itself the object of consciousness – that is, we can never observe ourselves carrying out the act of intellectual intuition. Instead, the theory of the self-positing subject must be understood as an attempt to articulate the underlying structure, the *Grundstruktur*, that informs consciousness but is not immediately apparent to it. Although the route to this goal cannot simply bypass the facts of consciousness, it must also lead beyond them, and this it can accomplish only through philosophical argument.[34]

33. SW, I, p. 464.
34. The reader should be aware that this claim as to the need for a *philosophical* grounding for the thesis of intellectual intuition is difficult to square with everything Fichte says on the topic. For example, in the same passage in which the previous quotation occurs, he also makes the following, apparently

Fichte's response invites a second, more difficult question: What precisely are these arguments that allegedly lead philosophy to Fichte's conclusions about the self-positing subject? In the preceding section we examined the theoretical considerations that led Fichte to develop his conception of self-awareness as immediate and nonrepresentational – namely, the need to avoid the infinite regress inherent in Reinhold's account of consciousness. In the present section, then, we shall concentrate on another central aspect of Fichte's theory, one that finds expression in the claim that an act of intellectual intuition, the subject's awareness of its own conscious activity, is an element of *every* conscious state.[35] Unfortunately, it is difficult to find passages where Fichte clearly articulates arguments that might support this basic claim. Nevertheless, I believe that his texts can be shown to suggest two distinct lines of argumentation. The first of these is a *phenomenological* argument that proceeds from a consideration of certain "facts of consciousness," namely, the experience of the "I think" in reflective self-consciousness; the second line of argumentation is *transcendental* in nature and is intimately bound up with Kant's own argument for the claim, central to the first *Critique,* that self-consciousness is a necessary condition for the possibility of experience.

As we have seen, Fichte explicitly rejects the possibility that his account of intellectual intuition can be established in a direct manner by simply "finding" this act itself as a fact of consciousness. Yet at times Fichte seems to contradict this view and to suggest a more straightforward grounding of his position. In a number

contradictory claim: "Neither the fact that there is such a faculty of intellectual intuition, nor what that faculty is, can be developed out of concepts. Everyone must find it immediately in himself, or he will never become acquainted with it" (SW, I, p. 463). See also p. 435: "I want only to recall to memory what anyone who has taken even one good look into himself must have found long ago." This tendency is especially prominent in earlier texts where, under the influence of Reinhold, Fichte emphasizes that the first principle of philosophy, the principle of the self-positing subject, must be immediately obvious. Notice, though, that even here Fichte does not claim that the fact that intellectual intuition belongs to every state of consciousness can be known without a philosophical theory. I emphasize the latter aspect of Fichte's position, because it seems more interesting than the claim that arguing for the theory of self-positing is simply a matter of inspecting "the facts of consciousness."

35. That this is indeed Fichte's position is made quite clear by a number of passages, including the one cited above (p. 76), as well as SW, I, p. 463: "... this intellectual intuition occurs in every moment of consciousness."

of passages from both the first and second introductions he implies that a simple inspection of ordinary consciousness is sufficient to convince anyone of the reality of intellectual intuition: "No doubt it is possible, within the experience admitted by everyone, to demonstrate that this intellectual intuition occurs in every moment of consciousness."[36] I believe that Fichte is best understood here as meaning that the existence of intellectual intuition is demonstrable not because it can simply be found "within the experience admitted by everyone," but rather because the assumption of its existence in every instance of consciousness helps to make sense of a particular phenomenon that is a part of everyone's experience. The phenomenon of ordinary experience to be explained by the hypothesis of self-positing is, I shall claim, that of reflective self-consciousness.

On this view, one of Fichte's reasons for espousing the theory of the self-positing subject rests upon the claim that the unique features of explicit self-consciousness require the assumption of an implicit, immediate self-awareness as a constitutive part of all conscious states. The characteristics of reflective self-consciousness that are relevant here are what we might call its immediacy and universality. The latter feature consists in the fact that reflective self-consciousness is always a possibility for a subject and can be brought about whenever the subject chooses to make its own thinking the object of its attention. The immediate nature of reflective self-consciousness is best exhibited by considering the nature of the transition from a state of objective consciousness ("I perceive the wall") to an explicitly self-conscious one ("It's I who am perceiving the wall"). Although the second state clearly differs from the first in terms of its content, the move from the former to the latter does not proceed via an inference nor on the basis of some further intuition concerning myself as subject. This fact suggests that no new content of knowledge is acquired in the second instance but that what occurs in reflective self-consciousness is a transformation of my immediate and implicit self-awareness into a kind of knowledge about myself that has the form of an objective judgment: "It was I [i.e., this self-identical subject] who was perceiving the wall."[37]

---

36. SW, I, p. 463.
37. Sartre understands reflective self-consciousness as arising from a "consulting" and "reconstituting" of the "nonthetic memories" left behind by one's everpresent prereflective self-awareness (1957, p. 46).

Although this argument does lend a certain degree of plausibility to Fichte's position, it is clearly not the only justification to which he appeals in support of his view, for these phenomenological considerations are reinforced in Fichte's texts by a second, *transcendental* line of argumentation. Central to this second argument is a claim that, although cited earlier, has thus far remained unexplicated. As we have seen, in cataloguing the components of awareness that make up all representational states, Fichte says that intellectual intuition is a "necessary component by means of which consciousness first *becomes possible.*"[38] Other statements are made repeatedly throughout Fichte's texts that unambiguously claim that the subject's self-positing "makes possible" consciousness in general.[39] Statements such as these make it clear that, following in the tradition of Critical Philosophy, Fichte believes his theory of the self-positing subject to be supported by a kind of transcendental argument in addition to the phenomenological argument already considered. In other words, Fichte's view is that philosophy can do more than verify his conception of the subject phenomenologically; it can also show how this structure of subjectivity is *necessary* in the sense that, without it, consciousness itself would not be possible.[40] Fichte's general claim, then, will be that the intellectual intuition present in every conscious state constitutes one of the necessary conditions for the very possibility of consciousness. And, since intellectual intuition is for Fichte a kind of self-awareness, it is easy to see that his position must be related in some general way to Kant's argument that self-consciousness is a necessary condition for the possibility of experience. It is a far more difficult task, however, to figure out, on the one hand, exactly what role Fichte believed the subject's self-positing to play in the constitution of experience and, on the other, to determine the precise relation of this claim to Kant's arguments concerning the necessary conditions for the possibility of experience.

Perhaps the best way of finding answers to these questions is to focus first on the issue of the relationship of Fichte's transcendental argument to Kant's. Although Fichte nowhere provides a very explicit answer to this crucial question, it should be possible to

---

38. SW, I, p. 473, my emphasis.
39. See, e.g., SW, I, pp. 91, 459, 462, 466, 521. Also GA, IV.2, p. 31.
40. This is an important respect in which Fichte's account of self-consciousness differs from Sartre's, for the latter does not make the transcendental claim that prereflective self-awareness is a necessary condition for the possibility of consciousness.

reconstruct the logic behind his position by taking a closer look at his references to Kant and at those passages of the first *Critique* to which he appeals for support. Of particular importance to this reconstructive enterprise is a rather long passage from the "Second Introduction to the *Wissenschaftslehre*" in which Fichte explicitly locates the roots of his own doctrine of intellectual intuition in Kant's theory of pure apperception. Included here is Fichte's significant remark that "the intellectual intuition of which the *Wissenschaftslehre* speaks . . . is not given a name by Kant, unless, if you will, by the expression 'pure apperception'."[41] The remainder of this passage makes it quite clear that Fichte regards his own position not only as *consistent* with Kant's, but as an *essential* part of it as well. That is, the theory of the self-positing subject is claimed to be already contained within the account of the subject given by Kant in the *Critique of Pure Reason*.

Unfortunately, Fichte does not distinguish very carefully between two distinct ways in which his position might be regarded as an essential part of Kant's own. In some places he seems to take the view that the theory of the self-positing subject is already developed by Kant himself and can be shown to be present in Kant's texts, even if it is couched in terms somewhat different from his own. He says at one point, for example, that "in Kant we find a very precise concept of the *pure I*, which is exactly the same as the one asserted by the *Wissenschaftslehre*."[42] Moreover, much of Fichte's actual treatment of those Kantian texts to which he appeals seems to imply this understanding of his relationship to his predecessor.[43] On this view, the doctrine of the self-positing subject is simply the outcome of a correct *interpretation* of Kant's texts; arriving at it requires only a proper understanding of Kant's doctrines, not a genuine development of them. At other times, however, Fichte suggests that his relationship to Kant is somewhat more complex. The implicit claim here is that his conception of subjectivity actually adds something to Kant's in the sense that it is a *necessary implication* of Kant's position, though not one that Kant himself recognized. On this interpretation, the fact that Kant never actually espouses an explicitly Fichtean charac-

---

41. SW, I, p. 472. The entire passage in question is found on pp. 471–7.
42. SW, I, p. 476.
43. See, e.g., his remark at SW, I, p. 476: "We shall not merely reason (*folgern*) here, but will cite Kant's own words."

terization of the subject is due not to a substantive disagreement between the two accounts, but rather to Kant's failure to grasp the full implications of his own most fundamental views on the subjective conditions required for the possibility of experience.

It is worth noting here that Fichte's claim to be articulating an essentially Kantian conception of the subject possesses a significance that extends well beyond our immediate goal of understanding Fichte's view. For the way in which Fichte understands and uses Kant is of great relevance to the larger historical question concerning the relationship between Kant's Critical Philosophy and the philosophical movement that succeeded it, nineteenth-century Idealism. At issue here is Idealism's claim, central to its own self-conception, to be primarily a development *immanent* to Kantian philosophy, one that aims, not to repudiate Kant, but to extend and thereby complete the Critical project. Since a large part of both Schelling's and Hegel's conceptions of the task of Idealism are derived from Fichte's own appropriation of Kant, the question as to the precise nature of the link between Kant and Fichte is of no little significance to making sense of Idealism's claim to be carrying on the Critical enterprise. Especially relevant here are those aspects of Idealism that purport to be motivated primarily by the need to work out the implications of Kant's own arguments concerning the nature of self-consciousness and the importance of the subject's self-relation for the constitution of experience.[44] Hence, it is important for our understanding of Fichte's theory, and for any attempt to assess the degree of continuity between Kant and his successors, that an answer be found to the question of why Fichte thought that his theory of the subject constituted an essential part of Kant's own position. Yet, as we shall see, specifying the nature of this relation turns out to be a task of considerable difficulty.

As a first step toward settling this issue, it is necessary to remind ourselves of an obvious, and crucial, difference between Fichte's theory of self-positing and the view of self-consciousness that is generally attributed to Kant. As we have seen, this difference does not lie in Fichte's assertion that self-awareness is to be understood

---

44. Pippin (1989) provides a sustained interpretation of Hegel that attempts to follow up precisely this connection. That is, Pippin tries to understand Hegel's thought as a project that consists primarily in drawing out the implications of some of Kant's basic positions, including, most centrally, the doctrine of apperception.

as a kind of intellectual intuition, since, as he himself points out, the characteristics he attributes to intellectual intuition are essentially consistent with those ascribed by Kant to the "I think." Rather, the important difference resides in Fichte's claim that this intellectual intuition – the subject's awareness of itself – is a constitutive part of *every* state of consciousness. As is well known, Kant's explicit position, as it is laid out in the transcendental deduction of the *Critique*'s second edition, is that, although self-consciousness must always be a *possibility* for the conscious subject, it is not for that reason always *actual:* "The 'I think' must [only] *be able* to accompany all of my representations."[45]

The key to assessing the extent to which Fichte's position is genuinely Kantian lies, I believe, in understanding the reasons for Fichte's apparent divergence from Kant on this fundamental issue. How is it that Fichte, without much comment, comes to espouse a view that, at first glance anyway, is so obviously at odds with Kant's own? If we return to the problem of self-consciousness with which the present interpretation began, we find that this distinctive position of Fichte's is already implicit in his formulation of that problem. It will be recalled that the specter of an infinite regress arose for Fichte as a result of two assumptions inherited from Reinhold: first, that every representation is related in consciousness to the subject and, second, that all consciousness conforms to the subject–object structure characteristic of representation. Hence, it would seem that the very way in which Fichte's problem is formulated assumes rather than argues for the assertion that a kind of self-awareness is involved in every conscious state. Since the source of this assumption is easily identified as Reinhold's theory of representation, it is tempting to conclude that Fichte's divergence from Kant on this issue is to be attributed to a careless misunderstanding of Kant's position that was widely shared by his immediate successors. This conclusion, however, is untenable, for there exists clear evidence that Fichte was fully aware of Kant's weaker claim that the "I think" must only *be able* to accompany all of a subject's representations. In Fichte's attempt to draw an explicit connection between the theory of self-positing and Kant's doctrine of pure apperception he quotes this very claim of Kant's: "What is the condition of the original unity of appercep-

45. "Das: *Ich denke,* muß alle meine Vorstellungen begleiten *können,*" KRV, B131, Kant's emphasis.

tion? According to §16 [of the *Critique of Pure Reason*] it is the following: 'that my representations *can* be accompanied by the: *I* think.' "[46] Fichte's citation of Kant, and especially his emphasis of the decisive word *können*, effectively rule out the possibility that the basis for Fichte's position is simply a careless reading of Kant. But how, then, might Fichte have arrived at his claim that *every* state of consciousness involves an element of immediate self-awareness?

In the following paragraphs I shall try to answer this question by examining the way in which Fichte attempts to use the arguments of the transcendental deduction to provide his own theory with a transcendental grounding. That is, I shall attempt to uncover whatever Critical arguments there might be in Fichte's texts for his claim that an intellectual intuition necessarily accompanies every conscious state. Before turning to the details of those texts, however, it may be helpful to sketch out the general nature of Fichte's argument: Much of what Kant says about the "I think," including his assertion that it is only a necessary *possibility*, is to be understood as referring to the *explicit* ascription of one's representational states to oneself that takes place in reflective self-consciousness. But this aspect of Kant's position must not be regarded as exhausting his account of self-consciousness. Rather, the logic of Kant's position commits him as well to a recognition of the subject's immediate relation to itself in *all* of its conscious states and therefore to a position very much like the theory of self-positing. Moreover (Fichte sometimes claims), not only is Kant logically committed to such a theory, but its basic tenets can even be found articulated in his texts, alongside the better known doctrine of the "I think" referred to above. (Recall here Fichte's assertion that Kant's notion of the pure I "is exactly the same as the one asserted by the *Wissenschaftslehre.* ")

Fichte's attempt to portray the subject's immediate self-awareness in all of its conscious states as a necessary condition for the possibility of consciousness takes the form of an exposition with commentary of Kant's own argument in the transcendental deduction concerning the necessary features of subjectivity. The implicit point of such a procedure, of course, is to show that Kant's own view of the I, if correctly understood, turns out to be identical to the notion of the self-positing subject. Fichte begins his account of the transcendental deduction by rehearsing Kant's point that the

46. SW, I, p. 475, Fichte's emphasis.

"original unity of apperception" constitutes the fundamental condition for the possibility of any consciousness whatsoever. He then asks what the condition of this unity of apperception itself is. Since Fichte explicitly equates 'unity of apperception' with 'identity of consciousness,'[47] his question here must be understood as asking what condition must hold if consciousness is to possess the most elementary unity it requires, namely, that all of its representations belong to one consciousness. In response to this question Fichte invokes Kant's doctrine of the "I think": This most basic unity of consciousness is possible only on the condition that all of my representations be recognizable as belonging to a single, self-identical subject of consciousness – in other words, that they all be accompaniable by the "I think." Fichte then goes on to ask what kind of a subject this doctrine of the "I think" requires:

> Which "I" is being spoken of here? That, perchance, which the Kantians blithely piece together from a manifold of representations, in none of which it was contained individually, though it is present in all of them together; so that the above-cited words of Kant would mean *this:* I, who think D, am the same I who thought C and B and A, and only through the thinking of my manifold thinking do I become an I for myself, namely that which is *identical* in the manifold? In that case Kant would be just as much a miserable babbler as the said Kantians; for then, according to him, the possibility of all thinking would be conditioned by another thinking, and by the thinking of this thinking, and I should like to know how we are ever to arrive at any thinking whatsoever![48]

Beneath the polemical tone of this passage lies a philosophical point that we must now try to understand. In its most general form Fichte's point can be characterized as the claim that, from Kant's perspective, and in contrast to the view of the majority of so-called Kantians, the I must be understood as more than a construct, the consciousness of which emerges only *after* actual experience and that consists in an awareness of the subject as simply "that which is identical in the manifold." It is important to note straightaway that Fichte does not *reject* this characterization of the I. On the contrary, it is precisely this – the identity of the subject with respect to its diverse representations – that we are aware of in reflective self-consciousness. Fichte's point must be, rather, that this account of the I cannot be taken as the whole of

47. SW, I, pp. 475–6.   48. SW, I, p. 475.

Kant's theory of the subject, and the reason given for this in the passage cited here is that such a conception of the subject is insufficient to account for "the possibility of all thinking," or, in other words, the possibility of consciousness. But what does this account of the I as "that which is identical in the manifold" leave out, thereby rendering the possibility of consciousness inexplicable? A clue to what Fichte thinks is omitted here is provided by his next statement, a citation of Kant's claim that the "I think" is an act of spontaneity rather than something that is given to or found within inner sense. Thus, the view of the I as simply the subjective correlate of the unity of the manifold of experience omits a crucial component of Kant's theory, according to which the subject is not merely a byproduct of the unity of consciousness but a spontaneous activity as well. Furthermore, this spontaneity of the I is essential to Kant's theory, for it is this activity that is in some way responsible for actually *bringing about* the conditions of unity upon which the possibility of consciousness depends. The account of the subject as *merely* "that which is identical in the manifold" turns the I into something that is conditioned by the very thing it (the subject) is supposed to be the condition of. The basic unity of consciousness that makes it possible for the subject to recognize its own self-identity throughout diverse representational states is not simply *given* in Kant's view; it is *produced* by the synthetic activity of the subject itself. Thus, the I is not merely *encountered* within consciousness; it is what actually *unites* its representations with one another, thereby establishing the fundamental unity of consciousness upon which the awareness of the identity of the subject of thought depends.

Thus far there is nothing problematic about Fichte's construal of Kant's doctrines, including his point that something more must be said about the subject in order to account for the possibility of consciousness in general. What we have not yet understood, however, is why that "something else" must be filled in by Fichte's own conception of the subject, including the view that an element of self-awareness belongs to every representational state. Immediately after the passage discussed earlier, Fichte cites and comments on a statement of Kant's that he clearly regards as support for this view:

"I call [the 'I think'] pure apperception ... because it is that self-consciousness which, in bringing forth the representation 'I think' (which must be able to accompany all other representations and *which is one and the same in all consciousness*), cannot itself be accompanied by any other representation." Here the nature of pure self-consciousness is described. It is the same in all consciousness.[49]

Fichte's singling out of Kant's statement that pure apperception is "one and the same in all consciousness" is obviously intended to convince us that Kant himself held something like Fichte's view that a kind of self-awareness accompanied *all* states of consciousness. But merely citing an isolated remark of Kant's – one that, after all, is capable of supporting other interpretations as well – fails to tell us *why* Fichte might have believed his view to be necessary for Kant's doctrine, especially when in so many other places Kant explicitly insists that self-consciousness must always be only a necessary *possibility*. Therefore, we are still left with the crucial question: Why must an account of the conditions of the possibility of consciousness include the assumption of a subject with an immediate self-awareness in each state of consciousness?

In this and other passages Fichte frequently associates the principle of self-positing with "the identity of consciousness," suggesting that this activity of the subject is supposed to play some crucial role in securing the *unity* of the I.[50] Unfortunately, it is extremely difficult to flesh out the details of this still very general claim. The most natural way of understanding Fichte's position is to take him to be claiming that the *unity of consciousness* is possible only on the assumption of a subject that stands in some relation to *all* of its representations. The strategy of this argument would be to identify this necessary relation with the self-awareness that Fichte characterizes as self-positing, or intellectual intuition. Hence, the latter would be understood as the subjective activity that establishes the unity among representations required for the

49. SW, I, p. 476. The citation of Kant comes from KRV, B132. Not only does Kant say here that self-consciousness is the same "in all consciousness," but he also seems to distinguish pure apperception from the awareness of the "I think" when he says that the former is that self-consciousness which *generates*, or "brings forth" (*hervorbringt*), the "I think." It is possible that this formulation also played a role in leading Fichte to think that Kant postulated an original, pure species of self-consciousness in addition to the explicit ascription of representational states to oneself. This suggestion is supported by Fichte's emphasis in the same passage of the distinction between "pure apperception" (i.e., self-positing) and "empirical" apperception, which he associates with the awareness of the I as "that which is identical in the manifold."

50. The other passages referred to include Section 1 of WL 1794, where self-positing is characterized as "I = I" (SW, I, p. 94; see also p. 107).

possibility of consciousness. This interpretation, however, raises a perplexing question: How could such a position be regarded as an essential part of Kant's own account of the apperceptive subject? If there is a basis in the first *Critique* for such an understanding of the conditions of the unity of consciousness, then perhaps it is to be found in Kant's claim (at B133) that the "analytic" unity of apperception – the awareness of the unity, or identity, of consciousness – is itself possible only on the hypothesis of some prior, "original" synthesis that actually *establishes* the connections among representations and makes the analytic unity of apperception possible. In other words, Kant's doctrine of original synthesis attributes to the subject an active role in *producing* the conditions of the unity of consciousness, conditions that make possible the subject's ability to become aware of its identity throughout its manifold representations. Furthermore, Kant himself points out that *all* of my representations, not merely those with respect to which I become explicitly self-conscious, must be subject to this original synthesis, for otherwise they would not all belong to my consciousness and would "be nothing to me."

Thus, the theory of the self-positing subject might be understood as an attempt to specify the nature of this original synthetic activity.[51] It is obvious that the self-ascription of conscious states through the "I think" cannot itself be what *establishes* the unity among all of my representations, since, on Kant's own account, the "I think" is not always actual – that is, not every representation is, in fact, accompanied by an explicit "I think." In other words, the unity of consciousness does not first come about when I reflectively attach the "I think" to a representation; rather, that unity must already exist in some sense before the act of explicit self-ascription can be carried out. From this consideration Fichte seems to conclude that representations can become part of a unified consciousness only insofar as each one enters into a kind of relation to the subject of awareness, and it is precisely this relation that the notion of intellectual intuition is meant to capture. Thus, Fichte's theory of self-positing can be seen as an attempt to give an account of the subjective conditions that must hold in order that all of a subject's representations can belong to a single consciousness. The activity of self-positing, then, would play the unifying

---

51. This account of Fichte's position is based, very roughly, on the interpretation put forth by Benson (1974, Chap. 3).

role attributed by Kant to original synthesis and would consist in a kind of relation between subject and representation, a relation understood by Fichte to be consciousness's immediate, prereflective awareness of itself as the subject of its conscious states. On this view, the "I think," as an explicit recognition of my self-identity in the face of diverse representations (or what I have earlier called "reflective self-consciousness") must always be *possible* with respect to each of my representations. But, Fichte would add, this "necessary possibility" of reflective self-consciousness itself depends upon the unity among my representations that intellectual intuition in each case establishes.

Although, as I have indicated, Fichte sometimes seems to regard his account of intellectual intuition as implied by Kant's position in the direct manner sketched above, this view is beset by a serious problem: As reconstructed here, the justification for Fichte's position depends upon its claim to be an essential, if perhaps implicit, component of Kant's doctrine in the transcendental deduction, yet this claim can be shown to rest upon a serious misunderstanding of the deduction's strategy. The import of Kant's crucial claim that the analytic unity of apperception necessarily presupposes a more fundamental synthetic unity of the manifold is *not* to suggest that the subject must therefore stand in some original relation to each of its representations that precedes its ability to recognize them as its own through an explicit attaching of the "I think." Kant's conclusion, rather, is that the unity of apperception is itself possible only on the presupposition that a condition of synthesis exists *among* the subject's representations themselves – or, more precisely, that those representations are synthesized in accord with rules that Kant identifies later in the deduction as the categories of the understanding. The point of Kant's argument here is to show that the *subjective* unity, or identity, that is involved in self-consciousness is possible only on the presupposition of a kind of *objective* unity. The condition, referred to by Kant, under which *all* representations must stand if they are to be united within a single consciousness turns out not to be a relation between the subject and each of its representations but an activity of synthesis that establishes objective connections among the subject's representations themselves.[52]

52. That Fichte may have actually misunderstood Kant in this way is suggested
    by the fact that his discussion of the conditions of the unity of consciousness

What we must conclude from all of this is that Fichte's claim that intellectual intuition necessarily accompanies every representational state cannot be justified simply by pointing to Kant's arguments in the transcendental deduction. If there is a transcendental grounding for this view, it must be supplied by Fichte himself. What looks most like an argument for this position is formulated by Fichte in a single statement located several pages before the treatment of apperception referred to previously. There Fichte says that sensible intuition "is possible only in combination with intellectual intuition, since everything that is to become *my* representation must be related to me" (presumably through intellectual intuition).[53] On a first reading this claim seems plausible enough, but it quickly loses its initial intuitive force when we recall that Kant gave an alternative account of the conditions that must hold for a representation to be "my own," one that does not require each of my representations to be related to me in the Fichtean manner: In order for representations to count as mine, I must *be able* (reflectively) to recognize them as belonging to a single unitary consciousness. What makes this condition possible for Kant is not an original, immediate awareness of each of them as my own, but the joining together of these representations in accord with the categories, a synthesis that establishes the minimal degree of connectedness among the contents of empirical consciousness required for the subject's recognition of its own identity. What would be needed, then, to convince us that Fichte's position is a genuine extension of the Kantian view is an independent argument showing that the synthesis of representations effected by the categories is by itself insufficient to account for the possibility of self-consciousness. But if there is such an argument to be found in Fichte's texts, it is a deeply buried one indeed. In what follows I shall point out two short passages that hint at something like the desired argument and then make some brief and tentative suggestions as to how these remarks might be understood.

The first of these passages appears in a footnote to the passage cited earlier in which Fichte discusses apperception and Kant's account of the conditions of experience:

at SW, I, pp. 475–7, completely ignores the crucial role that the synthesis of representations according to the categories plays for Kant in ensuring the objective unity (among representations) required for the analytic unity of apperception.

53. SW, I, p. 464.

> Through the joining together of various representations there would emerge only a manifold *thinking* (*ein mannigfaltiges Denken*), as *one* thinking in general, but by no means would there emerge something that thinks (*ein Denkendes*) within this manifold thinking.[54]

Here Fichte does appear to be claiming that the establishment of objective connections *among* one's representations in accord with the categories ("the joining together of various representations") is itself insufficient to explain the possibility of self-consciousness. What is both interesting and puzzling about this passage is that whereas he admits that the synthesis effected by the categories is capable of yielding a unity of consciousness ("*one* thinking"), he denies that this unity alone constitutes a sufficient condition for self-consciousness. What this merely objective synthesis cannot account for, we are told, is the awareness of a *thinker* of those representations (*ein Denkendes*).

A similar line of thought is expressed in the paragraph to which the footnote just cited is appended. Although we have quoted this passage once before, let us recall a portion of it, this time with the relevant points given special emphasis:

> Which "I" is being spoken of here? That, perchance, which the Kantians blithely piece together from a manifold of representations, *in none of which it was contained individually, though it is present in all of them together;* so that the above-cited words of Kant would mean this: I, who think D, am the same I who thought C and B and A, and *only through the thinking of my manifold thinking do I become an I for myself,* namely that which is identical in the manifold?[55]

Fichte's objection to the conception of the I as merely "that which is identical in the manifold" is that it is committed to the (absurd) view that "I become an I for myself" only in retrospect, that is, only through "thinking" (we would say "reflecting on") previous instances of thinking. On this view, it is only through this thinking or reflecting that I come to recognize that "I, who think D, am the same I who thought C and B and A." But how can it be, Fichte

---

54. SW, I, p. 476n.: "So würde durch das Zusammenfassen dieser mehreren Vorstellungen doch nur ein mannigfaltiges *Denken*, als *Ein Denken überhaupt*, keineswegs aber ein Denkendes in diesem mannigfaltigen Denken herauskommen" (Fichte's emphasis).
55. SW, I, p. 475.

asks, that the I becomes present to itself when its representations are taken together, if it is not contained in any one of them individually? Is it plausible to conceive of the I as appearing for the first time in reflective self-consciousness without it already being present in some form in the individual representational states that are reflected upon?

Fichte's remarks in these two passages seem to rest upon the claim that there is more to the phenomenon of reflective self-consciousness than can be accounted for by the synthesis of representations according to the categories. Thus, it must be Fichte's view that self-consciousness involves more than the awareness of a unity among the representations of consciousness, more than simply an awareness of the numerical *identity* of consciousness (i.e., an awareness of the fact that all of my representations constitute a single thinking). In addition, self-consciousness is said to include an awareness of the subject *as subject*, that is, as "a thinking something." Another way of putting this would be to say that being conscious of myself as the single thinker of A, B, C, and D involves more than recognizing that A through D exist together within a single consciousness; it also involves an awareness of their being (or having been) represented, or present for a subject. Self-consciousness, then, would include as one of its elements an awareness of the subject's *subjectivity* – that is, an awareness of its *having* of representations, of its ongoing activity of representing. Thus, Fichte's implicit claim would be that this aspect of self-consciousness is not derivable from any merely objective features of consciousness, including the synthetic connections that necessarily hold among a subject's representations. Moreover, it is precisely this defect that Fichte apparently thinks can be remedied by his hypothesis of intellectual intuition: The explicit, reflective consciousness of myself as the *subject* of my diverse representational states is possible only insofar as such consciousness can draw upon prior, implicit awarenesses of my subjectivity, my having of representations, in each of those conscious states.

Whatever the merits of this reconstructed argument might be, it is important to note that it fails as a transcendental argument of the Kantian sort. What it is unable to show (or, perhaps, what we have failed to understand) is why the subject's immediate self-awareness in all of its conscious states is necessary if consciousness is to be possible. It is not enough simply to say, as Fichte sometimes does,[56] that if consciousness requires self-consciousness as one of its conditions, then whatever is involved in the constitution of self-consciousness must be regarded as a necessary condition of consciousness as well. For there may be universal features of the phenomenon of self-consciousness that are nonetheless not *necessary* in the transcendental sense. What must be shown if this transcendental claim is to succeed is that the aspect of self-consciousness under consideration – in this case, the alleged presence of intellectual intuition in all instances of representation – plays some indispensable role in the constitution of consciousness. What we must conclude, then, is that this aspect of Fichte's account of self-consciousness is the most difficult to reconcile with not only the letter but also the spirit of Kant's philosophy. This does not imply that Fichte's view is wrong. What it does mean is that the phenomenological considerations that motivate his position are ultimately more persuasive than his transcendental claim – and that, in this respect, Fichte's theory cannot be regarded as a genuine extension of Kant's account of the necessary conditions of experience.

Self-positing as self-constituting existence

At this point it is important to make clear that the foregoing account of self-positing as a species of self-awareness constitutes only a part of Fichte's theory of the self-positing subject. This will come as no surprise to anyone who is familiar with Fichte's texts, for on the basis of the interpretation put forth in the preceding two sections we are not yet in a position to understand some of the most distinctively Fichtean language associated with the doctrine of self-positing. Above all, we have not yet provided an explanation of Fichte's peculiar, but central claim that "the I posits itself unconditionally," nor have we understood what Fichte means when he employs the term *Tathandlung* to characterize the subject. We can understand this aspect of Fichte's theory only by examining a different set of questions that played an equally central role in motivating the development of the doctrine of the self-positing subject. This second set of problems revolves around the need to clarify the ontological status of the Kantian subject by providing an answer to the question, What kind of *being* is to be

56. See SW, I, pp. 459, 466, 525.

attributed to the subject? Or, alternatively, in what sense does the representing subject *exist*? In order to answer these questions we shall need first to uncover the nature of the problem of the existence of the I and then to examine the means by which Fichte attempted to arrive at a solution. The basic thrust of this solution can be expressed in general terms as the thesis that the subject's existence must be understood as fundamentally different from the kind of existence we attribute to things, and for this reason the concepts required for an adequate account of subjectivity will necessarily differ from those used to comprehend objects. The remainder of this section will be concerned primarily with spelling out more clearly what Fichte believed these fundamental differences to be. Once again, we shall gain access to the details of Fichte's theory by first examining the specific philosophical controversy out of which his view emerged.

Our attempt to understand this aspect of Fichte's theory leads us again to the *Aenesidemus* review, for it is here, in response to the question of the subject's existence, that we find the first use of the expression *Tathandlung,* a term later abandoned in favor of the language of self-positing. Although Fichte explicitly states that the doctrine of the *Tathandlung* "can be neither explained nor proved" in the *Aenesidemus* review itself, it is possible nevertheless to glean from this article an understanding of one of the important motivating forces behind the notion of the self-positing subject.[57] A starting point for such an understanding is provided by Fichte's claim, central to the review, that the absolute subject is not to be understood as a kind of thing in itself. Since this claim arises in the context of Fichte's response to Schulze's critique of Reinhold, it will be necessary to examine briefly the nature of that critique as it pertains to the issue of the subject's existence.

The problem of the type of existence to be attributed to the subject arises as part of the debate over how Kant's claim that the mind serves as the "ground" for its own conscious experience can be understood in a way that is consistent with Critical principles. Schulze begins his attack on this doctrine by setting out what both he and Reinhold take to be the central tenet of Kant's philosophy, namely, "that the ground (*Grund*) of a large part of the determinations of the objects of our representations is attributed to the nature of our faculty of representation (*Vorstellungs-Vermögen*) itself."[58] The term 'faculty of representation' derives from Reinhold's reconstruction of Kant and is defined by him in the following passage:

> The faculty of representation is that through which pure representation . . . is possible and that which must be present prior to all representation in the cause of representation, i.e., in that which contains the ground of the reality of pure representation. . . . The efficient cause, the ground of the reality of pure representation, is called the representing power. . . . This power is distinct from pure representation in the same way that every ground is distinct from its consequence, and every cause from its effect.[59]

Two important claims about the subject are contained in this notion of a faculty of representation: First, the subject ("the faculty of representation") exists prior to any particular instance of consciousness, and second, the subject plays a causal role in the constitution of consciousness in that it produces, or creates, its "pure representations" (i.e., the synthetic a priori components of its experience). Hence, Reinhold understands the faculty of representation as a kind of noumenal subject, a metaphysically real entity that exists prior to and independently of experience and that belongs to the realm of things in themselves. Analogous to the thing in itself, which, at least on some accounts of Kant's philosophy, supplies the objective content of sensation, Reinhold's faculty of representation is the efficient cause, or *Real-Grund*, of the subjective, a priori elements of experience. Moreover, the faculty of representation, like the noumenal object, is in principle incapable of being represented or known within experience, since it necessarily stands outside of experience as a condition of it.

Needless to say, Schulze has an easy time disposing of Reinhold's notion of the faculty of representation from within the perspective of Critical Philosophy itself. Two decisive objections are raised against Reinhold's view. The first is that this explanation of the a priori elements of experience misuses the category of causality, since the thesis that a noumenal faculty is the *cause* of its pure representations violates the fundamental Kantian principle

---

58. SW, I, p. 10. This is actually Fichte's own paraphrased version of Schulze's statement.
59. Reinhold (1790, I, pp. 175–6, 178). This passage is also cited in a similar context by Benson (1974, pp. 109–10).

according to which the theoretical validity of the categories is restricted to the realm of experience. Yet on Reinhold's view the subject necessarily stands outside all experience, and for this reason the category of causality cannot be employed to characterize whatever relation might hold between it and its conscious representations. The second objection has to do with Reinhold's implicit claim that philosophy can provide us with knowledge of the faculty of representation and of the role it plays in the constitution of experience. According to Schulze, the most that Critical Philosophy could claim to establish (and on his view it fails to accomplish even this) is that we are compelled to *think* of the mind as the ground for certain of its representations, but it is prevented by its own principles from claiming to *know* that this view in fact accords with reality.

Fichte recognizes the validity of Schulze's objections and yet is convinced that they do not really apply to Kant's philosophy if the latter is correctly understood. It is easy to see that the force of both of Schulze's objections relies upon Reinhold's assumption that the subject in its role of "grounding" experience is to be interpreted as a transcendent entity that serves as a kind of noumenal cause of the formal elements of consciousness. It is no surprise, then, that Fichte's first move in his defense of Kant is to deny that the subject is a kind of thing in itself. This is certainly part of the point made in the well-known passage from the *Aenesidemus* review in which Fichte charges that Schulze, "as soon as he hears the word 'faculty of representation,' can think of nothing other than some kind of thing (round or rectangular?) which exists *independently* of *its representing* as a thing in itself, more specifically, as a thing which represents (*ein vorstellendes Ding*)."[60] As this early passage indicates, Fichte's point involves more than the claim that the subject is not a thing in itself; it is not a *thing* in any sense whatsoever. That is, it is not enough to point out that the subject cannot be coherently understood as having a noumenal existence; it must also be recognized that the categories that apply to empirical objects – substance and causality – are equally inappropriate for understanding the nature of subjectivity.

While it is clear that Fichte's response to Schulze indicates the general direction in which a defender of Critical Philosophy must go, it is less obvious how precisely the subject is to be understood

60. SW, I, p. 11.

so that one avoids the thesis of a noumenal subject while still allowing for the mind to "ground" experience. This challenge, the very one taken up by Fichte, is implicitly posed by Schulze's criticism of Kant, which is articulated in the following passage:

> In the *Critique of Pure Reason* Kant never clearly and expressly explains how one is to think of the subject from which the necessary elements of our knowledge are supposed to originate. . . . He never states, in any of those passages where he presents representations and principles as originating from the mind, what this mind really is that according to him is to be thought as the source of certain components of our knowledge.[61]

Schulze's ultimate conclusion is that it is no mere accident that the fundamental question raised here ("what this mind really is") is left unanswered by Kant. Although Reinhold's conception of a faculty of representation is naive and contradictory, Schulze attributes this not to a lack of acuity on Reinhold's part but rather to the fact that he attempts to answer a question that is in principle unanswerable from Kant's perspective. Schulze tries to show that this is so by considering what he takes to be an exhaustive list of the alternatives open to Critical Philosophy. He asks whether the mind, or "the subject of representations,"[62] is to be understood as a thing in itself, a noumenon, or a transcendental Idea and then goes on to reject each of these candidates in turn. We might add to Schulze's list Kant's own point that the subject of consciousness cannot be a kind of empirical object since, as Hume pointed out, we have no "impression," or sensible intuition, of it. Thus, a defender of Critical Philosophy is left with the following question: If the subject cannot be any of these possibilities, then what exactly is it?

The path that Fichte will ultimately follow is already hinted at in his rather obscure claim in the *Aenesidemus* review that the subject is to be understood not as a mere fact, a *Tatsache*, but as a *Tathandlung*, a "fact-act." In creating this new term for the subject Fichte starts with the word *Tatsache* but replaces *Sache* ('thing') with *Handlung* ('act'), thereby expressing what will become the central point of his theory of the subject: The I is not to be under-

---

61. Schulze ([1792], 1911, p. 125).
62. That Schulze ([1792], 1911) equates 'mind' with 'the subject of my representations' is made clear on p. 121.

stood as a thing but as an activity. Furthermore, the subject is a
"*Tat*"-*handlung,* an activity that is at the same time a deed, or fact.
The point of joining *Tat* with *Handlung* to coin a new term for the
subject is to suggest that the existence of the I, its facticity, stands
in some intimate relation to its activity and, further, that it is
this relation that essentially distinguishes a subject from a thing.
Whereas in the preceding sections we examined the nature of the
fundamental activity that Fichte attributes to the subject (its
immediate intuition of itself in its own conscious states), our
present concern is to understand more precisely how he conceives
of the relationship between this activity and the subject's existence. Unfortunately, merely creating a new philosophical term
still leaves us a long way from a fully articulated account of this
relationship. After all, an analysis of the term *Tathandlung* does not
itself enable us to understand the precise way in which the *Tat,* the
existence of the I, is related to its *Handlung,* or activity. One question that it leaves unanswered is whether the subject is to be
regarded as a result – or product – of its own activity, or whether
it is to be identified with its activity, such that it simply *is* its
activity and nothing else.

One central passage from the WL 1794 lends strong support to
the first of these interpretations: "[The I] is at once the agent (*das
Handelnde*) and the product of the action (*das Produkt der Handlung*), that which is active (*das Tätige*) and that which is produced
by the activity."[63] This formulation seems to imply that in characterizing the I there are two things to be distinguished from each
other – the subject's activity and the result of that activity – and
that the I is somehow to be identified with each of these. If understood in this way, however, Fichte's view seems to raise more
questions than it answers. The most obvious question is how we
are to envision the subject as both activity and product of that
same activity. Apart from the logical difficulties involved in *identifying* the subject with two distinct things, one is left wondering
precisely what this subject is that is supposedly produced by the
active I. If the distinction intended is one between the I as a pre-
conscious "transcendental activity" and the I that is produced by
this activity and known within experience, then one simply
recommits Reinhold's error of understanding the subject as a noumenal cause that operates prior to experience in the production of
a part of that experience.

63. SW, I, p. 96.

Fortunately, there is another way of understanding this claim of Fichte's that avoids these problems and that fits more closely with his other attempts to characterize the existence of the I in terms of its activity. The principal difficulty of the previous formulation stems from its use of the language of "production." This metaphor is fundamentally misleading, for it encourages us to think of the subject's activity in terms analogous to those that apply to actual constructive activities, such as the building of a house or the making of a shoe. In the latter case, it is meaningful to distinguish product from productive activity for the simple reason that a shoe, once created, acquires an existence that endures independently of any shoe-making activity. But if we recall the preceding account of the I's activity as intellectual intuition, that is, as the subject's constant and immediate awareness of itself as conscious, it becomes clear that there is no meaningful analogy to be drawn between the production of things and the kind of activity that is characteristic of the subject. The reason for this is that in the case of intellectual intuition the activity at issue is inseparably bound up with its "object," with that which it "produces." Unlike activities involving real objects, the activity of self-positing does not "produce" in the sense of engendering a product that continues to exist apart from the activity that created it. The cessation of the I's immediate self-awareness leaves no trace or residue behind itself; in the absence of that intellectual intuition there is in fact no conscious subject "still there."

Hence, we must conclude that, on its most straightforward reading, Fichte's characterization of the subject as both product and activity is unsatisfactory. This may mean that this way of characterizing the I is simply misguided, or it may mean that we have failed to understand it correctly. Might there not be other kinds of production, different from the construction of real objects, in terms of which we could make more sense of Fichte's claim that the subject is both agent and product of its activity? Perhaps the sense of "production" we should have in mind here is more akin to that in which an electric current is said to be "produced by" the motion of electrons. In this case the current is nothing more than the motion of electrons, and yet it would not be unusual to say that their activity also *produces* the current. In other words, there is a sense in which the current both "is" and "is a product of" its own activity, and it seems to be along similar lines that Fichte wants to understand the relationship of the I's existence to its activity.

Thus, Fichte's claim that the I is "at once" agent and product of the same activity requires a notion of production in which the distinction commonly made between activity and product does not apply. This same idea, however, is formulated more clearly in the second of the two interpretations of the *Tathandlung* suggested previously. There the crucial point is stated quite explicitly: The subject simply *is* its activity. In fact, this formulation of Fichte's position is found in passages from a number of works, including the first published version of the *Wissenschaftslehre*. In articulating the first principle of philosophy in the WL 1794, Fichte provides the following account of the subject's existence:

> *That whose being or essence (Wesen) consists simply in the fact that it posits itself as existing* is the I as absolute subject. Insofar as it *posits* itself, it *is;* and insofar as it *is,* it *posits* itself. . . . *To posit oneself* and *to be* are, as applied to the I, perfectly identical.[64]

This passage explicitly takes the position that the subject is to be *identified* with its activity of self-positing, or, in other words, that the existence of the I consists in nothing more than its awareness of itself as representing. It is not merely that the "I am" can be *inferred* from the "I think"; rather, the two propositions are to be understood as expressing the same content. To be aware of oneself as thinking is already to exist as an I, and to be an I consists in nothing beyond such self-awareness. Not surprisingly, it is this second formulation of his view that Fichte retains and emphasizes even more strongly in later writings. Typical here is his statement from the first introduction that "for idealism the intellect is a *doing* (*ein Tun*), and absolutely nothing beyond that; one should not even call it *something active* (*ein Tätiges*), because this expression denotes an existing something in which activity inheres."[65]

It is clear from passages such as these that Fichte eventually abandons the potentially misleading language of his early formulation in favor of clearer statements of his position, which emphasize that the subject is neither a "something" that acts, nor a faculty with a power to act, but simply *is* the activity of self-positing. Fichte's rejection of the view of the subject as "an active

---

64. SW, I, pp. 97–8. In contrast to the Heath–Lachs translation, I have rendered 'Ich' as 'I' rather than 'self'.
65. SW, I, p. 440. 'Intellect' (*Intelligenz*) is here a synonym for 'I' or 'absolute subject'. See also SW, I, p. 495.

something" is clearly intended to circumvent the problems that plagued Reinhold's assumption that the faculty of representation has an existence prior to actual consciousness. In denying this assumption Fichte frees himself from the position, untenable for Critical Philosophy, of postulating a preexisting subject as the noumenal ground of its conscious states. But Fichte's identification of the subject with the activity of self-awareness entails more than a rejection of the notion that the subject exists prior to actual consciousness. For he also denies that the activity of self-positing *results* in the subject's acquiring any kind of being apart from that activity itself: "Self-positing does not produce some sort of existence (*Existenz*) of the I as a thing . . . persisting (*bestehen*) independently of consciousness."[66] Not only does the subject not exist prior to actual consciousness, it in no case comes to share one of the features characteristic of *things* (not just things in themselves, but empirical objects as well) – namely, that they go on existing independently of any consciousness of them. This point can be seen as a denial of the claim that subjectivity can be understood in terms of the concept of 'substance'.[67] That is, the subject is not to be conceived of as a kind of enduring, underlying substrate that "has" its representations in the way that a substance has properties. On the view Fichte espouses, the only way in which the subject can "have" representations is by being aware of them as its own, by referring them to itself through an act of intuiting, without which there would *be* no subject to apprehend.

It is not difficult to see that these claims are more or less direct consequences of Fichte's basic strategy of identifying the subject with the activity of self-positing. For if the I is nothing apart from its activity, and if that activity never occurs apart from actual instances of consciousness, then it must be concluded that the subject does not exist independently of its actual conscious states. This point is already expressed in the *Aenesidemus* review in Fichte's rejection of Reinhold's assumption that the subject exists "independently of its representing."[68] But there is more to Fichte's position than merely this. Since the fundamental activity of the subject, its self-positing, is a kind of self-awareness, it follows that not only is there no subject apart from actual consciousness, but also that there is no subject that is not *self*-aware. As Fichte

66. SW, I, p. 529.   67. GA, IV.2, p. 29.
68. "Unabhängig von seinem Vorstellen" (SW, I, p. 11).

expresses it in the WL 1794, "What does not exist for itself is not an I."[69] Self-awareness, then, is an essential feature of subjectivity without which there can be no subject at all.

In addition to the identification of the I with its self-positing activity and the related claim that self-awareness is an essential feature of subjectivity, there is a further aspect of Fichte's characterization of the subject's existence that we must now examine. In the beginning of this chapter we saw that, especially in his earlier writings, Fichte sometimes refers to the self-positing subject as "the absolute I." Before ending our treatment of his account of self-consciousness, we should attempt to understand in what sense the self-positing subject is "absolute." It should be obvious by now that Fichte does not intend to assert anything like the views most commonly attributed to him. His theory, for example, is manifestly *not* based upon the claim that the subject, in an original act of self-positing, creates itself, its world, and all of the determinations of that world. It should be equally obvious that Fichte does not intend 'absolute' to be understood as a synonym for 'noumenal', for he denies that the subject is a thing in itself capable of existing independently of actual consciousness. In what sense, then, is the subject absolute? A partial answer to this question is to be found by recalling the role that the self-positing subject allegedly plays in "grounding" consciousness. Although Fichte rejects Reinhold's conception of the faculty of representation as the noumenal cause of its synthetic a priori representations, he nevertheless ascribes a kind of grounding role to the subject with respect to its experience: As an intuiting activity immanent to consciousness, the subject's self-positing is viewed as grounding experience insofar as its intellectual intuition constitutes one of the conditions for the possibility of self-consciousness, without which consciousness itself would not be possible.

Yet the subject is absolute for Fichte in more than just the sense that the activity of self-positing is regarded as a necessary condition for the possibility of consciousness. A second sense is alluded to in the *Aenesidemus* review in rather mysterious statements such as the following: "The faculty of representation exists *for* the faculty of representation and *through* the faculty of representation."[70]

---

69. SW, I, p. 97.
70. SW, I, p. 11. Notice that Fichte refers to the absolute I as a *faculty* (of representation) only in this early text, before having fully developed the view that the subject must be understood as an activity rather than a capacity or faculty.

That the subject exists "for itself" clearly refers to the position mentioned before that the subject is necessarily self-aware. Although it is only implied in this quote, one could add to this the claim that the subject exists *only* for itself; that is, it ceases to exist in the absence of its own self-awareness and can exist, *qua* subject, only for itself, never for another conscious subject.

Yet how is it that the subject exists "through," or by means of, itself? This enigmatic claim is expanded upon in a later passage from the same text: "The mind . . . is a transcendental Idea which is to be distinguished from all other such Ideas by the fact that we realize it through intellectual intuition, through the 'I am' and, more specifically: 'I am simply because I am.' "[71] One of the points of this statement is to emphasize that the subject is unique among all entities in that it alone is "realized," or brought into being, through mere intuition. This itself constitutes a fundamental distinction between a subject and an object, for it is an essential characteristic of a thing, whether empirical or transcendent, that it cannot be brought into existence through the mere activity of consciousness. But there is apparently more to Fichte's claim than this, for the subject ("the faculty of representation") is said to exist "through itself"; in other words, the I is in some sense a *self-constituting* being. Fichte's *causa sui* language here is bound to strike us at first either as a retreat to a position that ascribes mystical or divine characteristics to the subject, or as committing him to a blatantly incoherent conception of the I as self-caused or self-created. Perhaps, however, a more sympathetic reading of this claim can be found that is also consistent with the foregoing analysis of the notion of self-positing. As we have seen, Fichte does not mean to claim that the act of intellectual intuition results in the creation of a subject that then exists, as objects do, independently of consciousness. Nor is the subject to be understood as the agent

71. SW, I, p. 16. One question this passage raises is whether Fichte really views the subject as a transcendental Idea in the Kantian sense. I would argue that he simply takes over this suggestion from Schulze and that it is merely an early, provisional characterization of the subject that is abandoned shortly thereafter. The passage itself explicitly draws a fundamental distinction between the absolute subject and Kant's Ideas, for the former, unlike the latter, is actually *realized*, or made real (although certainly not in the same sense in which objects could be said to be real). What the subject might be regarded as sharing with the Ideas is their absolute, unconditioned nature, although, as the present discussion implies, there are crucial differences here as well in the sense in which each is absolute.

of an activity that *brings about* its own existence. Rather, Fichte must be understood as holding that the I just *is* the activity of referring diverse representations to a single possessor of those representations. ("*To posit oneself* and *to be* are, as applied to the I, perfectly identical.") If the subject is identical with its activity, and therefore has no existence beyond that activity, then it follows that the subject is "realized" (in the only sense that a subject can "exist") solely through this conscious activity; it is only in or "through" the act of self-awareness that the subject comes to be.

If, however, Fichte denies that the subject preexists its self-positing as the agent of that activity, can the I really be said to constitute itself? The subject may very well be constituted by the activity of intellectual intuition, but in what sense is it *self*-constituting? Fichte's answer here, I believe, ultimately rests upon his (and Kant's) view of the spontaneous, unconditioned nature of subjective activities. Unlike the motion of electrons, which could also be said to constitute the electric current, the activity of self-positing that constitutes the subject is uncaused; it has no ground in anything external to itself. This feature of the I points to another sense in which subjectivity is to be understood as structured according to principles distinct from those that govern the world of objects. For neither the subject's existence nor the nature of its activity is bound by or explainable in terms of the principle of causality. In contrast to activities within the objective realm, the subject's self-positing is not the effect of some antecedent cause that produces it in accord with a universal and necessary law. It is both meaningless and futile to attempt to explain the subject's activity by postulating or searching for some prior cause that makes the activity of self-positing proceed as it does. The only possible "explanation" of the subject's activity is transcendental rather than causal. That is, the subject cannot be "understood" in the sense that its activity can be shown to be a necessary consequence of some antecedent ground. The understanding of subjectivity is limited to transcendental explanation that "understands" the subject by revealing the essential structure of its activity and by showing how such activity is a necessary condition for the possibility of consciousness.

At this point the account of self-consciousness put forth by the theory of the self-positing subject can be summarized in three distinct claims: First, throughout all of its states, consciousness not only is directed at something outside itself, an objective representation, but is at the same time inwardly directed as well; that is, in all of its conscious states the subject stands in a relation to *itself* that consists in an immediate, nonempirical awareness – an "intellectual intuition" – of its own conscious activity. Second, it is this conscious relation between subject and representation that accounts for the possibility of a unitary self-conscious subject and thereby constitutes a necessary condition for the possibility of consciousness in general. Finally, the I simply *is* its constant activity of self-awareness, and nothing more. As such, the subject is essentially self-relating (always aware of itself as subject) and self-constituting (ungrounded in anything that is not its own activity).

Having acquired an overview of his account of self-consciousness, we are now in a position to raise a question that has dominated much recent discussion of Fichte's thought: Can the theory of the self-positing subject be formulated without becoming entangled in a logical paradox?[72] This question is especially important, since what appears to be problematic in Fichte's conception arises at the most fundamental level of the theory, namely, in its attempt to define the I in terms of the activity of intellectual intuition. The problem here is not simply that Fichte regards the subject as a kind of activity but, rather, that the activity in which it is said to consist is an essentially self-referring one, a *self-*intuiting. In short, such an account seems to be hopelessly circular: How can a single entity be both the intuiter and that which is intuited *and*, at the same time, be identified with the intuiting activity itself?

Part of this mystery can be cleared up if we move beyond this very general way of formulating the problem and recall how Fichte actually characterizes the subject's distinctive activity. Above all, it is important to keep in mind the sense in which the intuiting under consideration is "reflexive." As we have seen, the I's self-intuiting is not to be understood as directed at some independently constituted object ("the self") that is distinguishable from that activity of intuiting. It is, rather, an awareness that is internal

---

72. The most influential discussion of this topic is found in Henrich's interpretation of Fichte (1982; also 1971, pp. 3–28). Henrich comes to the conclusion that the thesis of the self-positing subject is inherently paradoxical. Since his interpretation of Fichte's account of self-consciousness differs substantially from the one presented here, it is difficult in the present context to restate succinctly Henrich's account of the various forms in which the alleged paradox manifests itself. Nevertheless, the plausibility of the general claim that Fichte's position rests upon a logical paradox is easy enough to grasp without reproducing Henrich's objections in detail.

to the activity of consciousness itself, consisting in an awareness on the part of the conscious subject *that* it is aware. When articulated in this way, Fichte's theory loses some of its paradoxical appearance. There is nothing incoherent in the claim that consciousness is always aware of its own awareness – that, in other words, there is no such thing as "un-self-conscious" subjectivity.

Nevertheless, merely reminding ourselves of this point does not drive away all suspicion of paradox surrounding Fichte's position. On the contrary, it only enables us to formulate the problem more precisely. For, as we saw in the first section of this chapter, Fichte's understanding of the content of the subject's immediate self-awareness is not completely captured by the formulation just considered. That is, the subject's self-awareness is not merely the awareness that there is a representing going on, or even the awareness that there is a representing of a specific content X. Rather, the subject apprehends *itself* as representing; more precisely, in my self-positing I am aware of X as *mine,* as belonging to me. But this description of self-awareness, coupled with the claim that the subject does not exist apart from this awareness, yields a conception of the subject that, at the very least, is extremely difficult to grasp: On this view, the subject must be understood as an entity that simply consists in the activity of apprehending its representations as its own. Put in another way, the subject apprehends its representations as its own and exists only through that apprehending.

At this point I would like to propose a way of restating this apparently paradoxical claim that captures what I take to be Fichte's central point and articulates it in a somewhat less perplexing form: In the case of the subject's basic activity – its intellectual intuition – that which is apprehended (the mineness of a particular representation X) is not to be conceived of as preexisting the act of apprehending it. The claim here is not merely that my awareness of X as mine is a sufficient epistemic guarantee of its actually being so; the point is that X does not even exist as mine in the absence of such awareness. Thus, the relation between subject and representation that is apperceived in intellectual intuition does not itself *hold* independently of the I's intuiting of it.[73] Alternatively, there is no way for a representation to *be* mine apart from my intuiting it as such. The awareness involved in intellectual

73. Something like this point is suggested by Nozick's brief but helpful remarks on Fichte (1981, pp. 76, 89, 108).

intuition, then, must be understood as having the peculiar property of actually bringing about that which it is an awareness of. The implication of this view is that the subject of consciousness can be characterized only in terms that are bound to strike us as paradoxical: The I is essentially a self-referring activity that, only in referring to itself, is constituted as an existent.

We should not, I think, immediately conclude from this that Fichte's account of the subject is hopelessly paradoxical. Of course, the capacity for self-constitution that it ascribes to the subject violates the strictures to which empirical objects (understood as causally determined, extended substances) must conform. But this should not surprise us, for it is precisely this point – that the I cannot be understood as a kind of object – that underlies and motivates Fichte's basic project of attempting to grasp the essential structure of subjectivity. To insist that the subject be comprehensible in terms familiar to us from our knowledge of the objective world is to rule out from the beginning the possibility of attaining the comprehension we seek. At the very least, I would urge that we refrain from deciding whether Fichte has actually achieved this goal until we have seen his project carried out to completion. For the conception of the subject developed in this chapter will gain in plausibility if it can be shown that the same "paradoxical" structure attributed to the I of theoretical self-consciousness also informs practical subjectivity. It is precisely this claim that Fichte's theory of self-determination, the topic of our final chapter, aims to establish.

4

THE SELF-POSITING SUBJECT
AND PRACTICAL
SELF-DETERMINATION

In Chapter 2 we saw that Fichte's theory of subjectivity is best understood as one version of the project of demonstrating the unity of theoretical and practical reason. As such, the theory attempts to specify the essential feature of subjectivity in general by isolating a single, fundamental structure of consciousness that can account for the possibility of subjectivity in both its theoretical and practical forms. Furthermore, we saw that Fichte understands this structure as a particular kind of activity, which he terms "self-positing." The aim of Chapter 3 was to analyze Fichte's attempt to account for theoretical self-consciousness in terms of a subject's self-positing activity, and the task that faces us in the present chapter is to understand how Fichte intends to use the same notion as a principle of practical philosophy. In general terms, what Fichte must show is that practical subjectivity depends in an essential way upon self-positing activity, or upon the subject's entering into a kind of reflexive, nonobjective relation to itself, through which the subject also constitutes itself.

One important part of this project will be to specify the particular aspect of practical subjectivity that Fichte intends to give an account of. In doing so, it should first be pointed out that there are actually a number of ways in which Fichte attempted to draw an essential connection between theoretical and practical subjectivity.

One of the most widely known of these is expressed in remarks throughout the two 1797 introductions to the *Wissenschaftslehre* that refer to both pure apperception and the consciousness of the categorical imperative as kinds of intellectual intuition.[1] Such passages suggest the possibility of drawing an important parallel between theoretical and practical reason by showing that the practical subject's consciousness of its moral obligation is an immediate, nonrepresentational, and self-constituting kind of awareness and therefore similar to the self-positing involved in theoretical self-consciousness.

In this chapter, however, I shall examine only what I take to be the most philosophically promising of the connections that Fichte tried to draw between the theoretical and practical realms. As the title of this chapter indicates, my interpretation will focus primarily on Fichte's notion of self-determination. Within the Kantian tradition, of course, the notion of self-determination, or autonomy, is very closely linked to the categorical imperative and to issues of moral obligation. It is also possible, however, to conceive of self-determination more broadly, as a concept that might include but is not necessarily restricted to specifically moral forms of autonomy. Ultimately the principal aim of Fichte's practical philosophy was to defend something like Kant's own conception of moral autonomy. Yet the most interesting part of his discussion of self-determination takes place at a more abstract level of conceptual analysis, where the issue of greatest concern to him can be

---

1. SW, I, p. 472. There are other similar passages throughout the two introductions, among them the following piece from p. 466: "The intuition of self-activity and freedom is grounded in the consciousness of [the moral] law, which is undoubtedly not a derived, but an immediate consciousness. . . . Only through the medium of the moral law do I behold *myself*, and in beholding myself through it, I necessarily behold myself as self-active." The claim that I can grasp myself only through my awareness of the moral law is a provocative idea indeed, which, admittedly, my own interpretation of the link between theoretical and practical reason takes little account of. Is it possible to develop a coherent and sustained reconstruction of the position Fichte hints at here? Perhaps, although I myself do not see how it is to be done. The difficulty lies in making out the claim that *identifies* theoretical with practical spontaneity, or at least grounds the former in the latter. As I have argued in Chapter 2, it is not enough merely to point to the *active* nature of theoretical subjectivity in order to establish a deep connection between the theoretical and the practical. The activity of the theoretical subject is, or at least seems to be, of such a different nature from that of the practical subject that the burden falls on the proponent of such a position to explain more precisely how the two may be understood as identical, or in what sense the former is dependent upon the latter.

formulated in terms of the following questions: How is it possible to make sense of the notion of self-determination? For what kind of being is self-determination a possibility? This emphasis on the notion of self-determination is justified by the fact that it is regarded by Fichte himself as the most basic concept of practical philosophy. To be a practical being, for Fichte, is in very general terms to possess the capacity for determining oneself to act, as opposed to having one's actions determined by something external. Of course, this characterization of Fichte's view still leaves open the question of what precisely self-determination is and how it relates to self-positing. A preliminary articulation of this notion is found in his statement that the self-determining subject "is in every respect its own ground and *posits itself* unconditionally in a practical sense."[2] Two relevant points emerge from this statement: First, crucial to the concept of self-determination is the subject's ability to be, in some sense, "its own ground." Second, self-determination is to be understood as a form of self-positing. For now, we shall postpone a more precise analysis of 'self-groundedness' and turn instead to the relation between 'self-determination' and the more general notion of 'self-positing'.

Fichte's remark that self-determination involves self-positing "in a practical sense" is consistent with my claim that the concept of self-positing in Fichte's thought refers to a very general structure of consciousness that is somehow common to both theoretical and practical subjectivity. The role that the notion of self-positing is to play in Fichte's account of self-determination can be clarified by looking at his own characterization of the primary aim of his major work on ethics, *System of the Doctrine of Morals,* or, as I shall refer to it here, the *Sittenlehre.*[3] Toward the beginning of that work Fichte outlines his basic task by raising the following questions: Is it possible to develop a coherent conception of self-determination, one that elucidates what it means to be self-determined, in contrast to being determined by something external to oneself? And, what must be true of the practical subject in order to allow for the possibility of this self-determination? The answer Fichte gives can be formulated as follows: It *is* possible to arrive at a coherent conception of self-determination, but only if one starts with an

---

2. "Es ist in jeder Rücksicht sein eigener Grund, und *setzt,* auch in praktischer Bedeutung *sich selbst* schlechthin" (SW, IV, p. 38).

3. *Das System der Sittenlehre nach den Prinzipien der Wissenschaftslehre* (1798), GA, I.5, pp. 19–317; SW, IV, pp. 1–365.

adequate notion of the subject, that is, with one that recognizes the fundamental differences between a self and a thing, and thereby avoids the pitfall of thinking of the subject as a kind of object.[4] This is precisely what is supposed to be accomplished by the conception of the self-positing subject. In its most general form, then, Fichte's thesis will be that self-determination is a coherent possibility only for a *subject* – that is, only for an entity capable of entering into the kind of self-relation that he characterizes as a "self-positing." Since the principal aim of this chapter is to make sense of this basic project of Fichte's, it must involve not only an analysis of the notion of self-determination but also an examination of how the concept of the self-positing subject might be regarded as an essential foundation for a theory of self-determination.

In order to accomplish the latter goal we must first determine more precisely the content of Fichte's conception of the self-positing subject. Our analysis of this notion thus far has taken place in the context of theoretical self-consciousness, so we must now attempt to understand how the nature of the subject as it was articulated there might be relevant to an account of self-determination. First, we should recall that Fichte characterized the theoretical subject as an activity (rather than as a *faculty* for carrying out a subjective activity) and that this activity was simply a species of self-awareness. In Chapter 3 we saw that this position was intended in part as a rejection of Reinhold's view that the theoretical subject has a kind of (noumenal) existence prior to and apart from actual conscious experience. As we shall see in this chapter, Fichte's attempt to apply this view of the subject to the realm of practical subjectivity implies that he must provide an account of self-determination that does *not* invoke some notion of a noumenal agent. More specifically, Fichte must find a way of understanding self-determination that does not rely upon the hypothesis of a hidden, "true" self that exists outside of actual consciousness as the source of determinations for the agent's deeds in the empirical world.

A further aspect of the notion of self-positing subjectivity that will be relevant to Fichte's account of self-determination is the essentially reflexive nature of the subject's activity. This reflexivity is evident in the term 'self-positing', as well as in Fichte's description of the same as "an activity that returns into itself"

---

4. These questions, as well as the outline of Fichte's answer, are formulated most explicitly at SW, IV, pp. 34–6.

(*eine in sich zurückgehende Tätigkeit*). What these formulations are intended to express is that the distinctive feature of a subject, as opposed to a thing, consists in a kind of conscious relationship that it establishes to itself. Moreover, this self-relation is held to be of a very particular sort, which, as we saw in the case of theoretical self-consciousness, Fichte describes as "immediate," "nonrepresentational," and, further, as a relation in which "the agent and that which is acted upon are one and the same."[5] In the context of practical philosophy Fichte expresses this same point by denying that the relation the self-determining subject has to itself is one of "a passive looking on" (*ein leidendes Zusehen*).[6] This is to be taken to mean that the subject's relation to itself is not the same as its relation to an object of representational consciousness, where the object is thought to be there and to be constituted as it is independently of the subject's awareness of it. Rather, the subject's relation to itself – its self-positing – is a kind of conscious activity that, in both its theoretical and practical forms, *constitutes* the subject. We have already seen the sense in which, on Fichte's view, the subject constitutes itself in theoretical self-consciousness; our task now is to understand how, in "self-determination," this occurs for the practical subject as well.

Having made these preliminary points about the relationship between practical philosophy and the notion of self-positing, let us turn to the central question that faces us here: How does Fichte understand the notion of self-determination? Characterizing Fichte's position is made difficult enough by the existence of a number of distinct senses of self-determination in his texts, but it is complicated even further by the fact that he usually seems to be unaware of these crucial differences. For now it is sufficient to call attention to the most important of these distinctions, one between a weak and a strong sense of self-determination. In what follows I shall refer to these different conceptions as "formal" and "substantive" self-determination, respectively.[7] The former is treated

5. The latter formulation appears in the *Sittenlehre*, SW, IV, p. 22.
6. SW, IV, p. 32.
7. Although Fichte does not articulate this distinction in precisely the same form as I do here, my distinction is based upon Fichte's attempt to distinguish between "formal" and "material" freedom (SW, IV, pp. 135–56). My characterization of "substantive self-determination" is intended to capture the important features of Fichte's notion of "material freedom" and to spell out more clearly the differences he intended to assert between weak and strong self-determination.

in Fichte's account of willing in general under the name of "formal freedom." As we shall see, what Fichte has in mind here is close to Kant's conception of "practical freedom," or *Willkür*. To say that a subject's action is self-determined in this sense is merely to say that it is freely chosen, which further implies for Fichte that it is chosen in accord with a practical maxim. Although Fichte's texts are confusing on even this issue, I shall try to show that it is possible to extract from them a coherent and plausible account of this weaker notion of self-determination, and it is this task that we shall undertake first. Our examination of the stronger conception of self-determination will encounter interpretive problems of a significantly greater magnitude, for Fichte offers several distinct accounts of self-determination in this sense. In general terms, one could say that this second conception is intended to represent some notion of autonomy. At times Fichte clearly has in mind something close to Kant's account of moral autonomy, but I shall show that he also develops – or takes steps toward developing – a different conception of substantive self-determination, one that fits more consistently with his general theory of the subject as essentially "self-positing."

Since it is not immediately clear what these different accounts of substantive self-determination have in common that distinguishes them from formal self-determination, we should attempt at the outset to formulate this distinction more precisely. For Fichte any freely chosen act represents an instance of formal self-determination. That is, the subject is formally self-determined whenever it determines itself to act in accord with any practical maxim whatsoever. Substantive self-determination, on the other hand, requires that the subject also determine the maxims themselves according to which it acts. The intuition that lies behind this distinction is that to act on any subjective maxim is already to act freely, but that the subject is self-determined in an even deeper sense when it determines which maxims it wants to govern its actions. Furthermore, in order to be "substantively" self-determined, the adoption of one's maxims should involve more than merely arbitrary choice; it must proceed, rather, in accord with higher-level standards, or "norms," that spell out the criteria for which maxims the agent ought to adopt.[8] Finally, the subject is self-determined in a substantive sense only when these norms

---

8. Fichte uses the term 'norm' (*Norm*) in this context (SW, IV, p. 52), although I shall give it a somewhat more specific meaning than Fichte himself articulated.

themselves originate in a significant way from the subject itself. The central task of an account of substantive self-determination, then, will be to articulate in what sense the practical subject can be understood as the source of its own norms. We shall return to this issue, including a more careful consideration of the concept of a "norm," in our discussion of substantive self-determination. For now let us turn to a consideration of Fichte's account of formal self-determination.

Formal self-determination

In contrast to Kant's *Groundwork of the Metaphysic of Morals,* which opens with a consideration of the notion of a morally good will, Fichte's *Sittenlehre* begins with an extended analysis of "willing" (*das Wollen*) in general. The term 'willing' is intended here to have a fairly specific meaning in that it is distinguished from mere desiring or wishing, but it is also a quite general notion insofar as it is meant to encompass all of a subject's freely committed deeds regardless of their moral status. In other words, I "will" in both my moral and immoral actions, as well as when I choose to follow one morally neutral course of action over another. As Fichte makes clear in a later part of the *Sittenlehre,* the aspect of the will that he is attempting to characterize in his analysis of willing in general is nothing more than what he calls *Willkür,* which is understood to be the will's "capacity to choose," or its ability to "make a choice among several equally possible actions."[9] Although Fichte begins his moral theory with a consideration of *Willkür,* he does not at the same time explain what role it will play in his account of the ethical will. A clue to the connection Fichte intends to establish between the two is provided by his assertion that all willing involves a kind of self-determination – "a real self-determining of oneself by oneself."[10] Since we already know that self-determination will be the central category of Fichte's ethical theory, our first task must be to understand in what sense all willing involves for him a kind of self-determination.

As mentioned earlier, Fichte distinguishes between an instance of willing (*ein Wollen*), on the one hand, and merely having a desire, on the other. The main point of this distinction becomes clear

9. SW, IV, p. 159.
10. "Ein reelles Selbstbestimmen seiner selbst durch sich selbst" (SW, IV, p. 22). That he is referring here to *all* willing is made clear in other passages, e.g., p. 28.

when one considers that it is possible to experience a desire for a particular state of affairs without at the same time willing to act on that desire. What characterizes the latter state in distinction to the former is that willing involves, beyond merely having an incentive to act, a positive resolution (*Entschluß*) to pursue or to realize the object of one's desire.[11] Unlike sensuous drives and desires, this resolving to act is itself never given to the subject from without but requires instead the latter's own active participation. This capacity for transforming a mere incentive into a resolution to act is described by Fichte as constituting the will's "absoluteness" (*Absolutheit*),[12] which leads us to ask, In what sense is the will's resolving to act "absolute"?

An important part of Fichte's point is expressed in his frequently repeated claim that natural drives "have no causality upon the will's freedom," a claim that is expanded upon in the following statement: "Despite [the presence of] a drive I can determine myself in opposition to it; or, even if I determine myself in accord with the drive, it is still always I who determines me, never the drive."[13] The point that Fichte is making here is reminiscent of Kant's description of the will's "practical freedom" in the first *Critique,* according to which the will (*Willkür*) is *affected,* but not *determined,* by sensuous desire. The will is characterized there as practically free in the sense that "sensibility does not necessitate its action; rather, there is in the human being a capacity for determining oneself independently of any coercion by sensuous impulses."[14] Hence, the essential feature of the will's absolute nature consists, first, in its *Unbestimmbarkeit,* its "inability to be determined by anything external to itself,"[15] and, second, in the fact that it is free to determine which among the various incentives available to it will ultimately guide its action. This ability of the will to make a given incentive into a determining motive for action is regarded by Fichte as "absolute" in the sense that it is "something original (*ein Erstes*) which is grounded absolutely in itself and in nothing outside of itself."[16] As such, it "is not to be explained out of the influence of something that is external to the I, but solely out of the I itself."[17]

---

11. SW, IV, p. 159.   12. SW, IV, pp. 24–5.   13. SW, IV, p. 108.
14. KRV, A534/B562.   15. SW, IV, p. 28.
16. "Das Wollen, als solches, ist ein Erstes, absolut in sich selbst, und in nichts außer ihm Gegründetes" (SW, IV, p. 24).
17. SW, IV, p. 25. Moreover, it is made clear here that it is this feature of the practical subject that constitutes its *Absolutheit.*

This characterization of the will's ability to "determine itself," to determine which incentives will govern its actions, does not spell out precisely how this self-determination is to be understood. Does the will simply determine itself arbitrarily, or is there more to be said about the way in which the will resolves to act? Although Fichte does seem to ascribe to the will the ability to make arbitrary, ungrounded choices[18] (i.e., choices that are neither caused by natural processes nor made on the basis of a subjective reason), it is not this class of "blind" actions that is of most interest to him. Fichte's statement that one's willed acts are grounded in oneself is intended to refer not primarily to the subject's capacity for ungrounded choice but to a more articulated notion of self-groundedness. It is in the context of explaining the latter notion that Fichte introduces one version of the concept that will play a central role in his ethical theory, namely, the concept of reflection:

> By means of reflection . . . the individual tears himself away from the natural drive and makes himself independent of it (*stellt sich unabhängig von ihm hin*) as a free intelligence; he thereby obtains for himself the capacity to postpone the self-determination and, with this, the capacity to choose between various ways of satisfying the natural drive.[19]

As this passage makes clear, it is the subject's entering into a kind of relation to itself that accounts for the possibility of its "independence," or its capacity for formally free action. The self-relation at issue here is characterized as one between the reflecting I and the "natural drive" of the I, which in this context simply refers to the subject's immediate, given desires. What Fichte intends to express in the language of the "individual's tearing away from himself" is the idea that the subject is capable of stepping back and distancing itself from its immediate and perhaps only momentary desires, and that it is only under this condition that free choice becomes possible.[20] Yet *reflecting* upon one's desires,

18. The textual basis for this assertion is somewhat ambiguous, but Fichte does seem to allow for a class of actions that are free (in the sense of being spontaneous) and that do not conform to the characterization of formal freedom developed later as requiring purposive concepts and some degree of reflection. See, e.g., SW, IV, p. 178.
19. SW, IV, p. 179.
20. In the context of *formal* self-determination this stepping back from one's immediate inclinations does not require what one might call a "radical"

in the sense of merely being aware of them, is obviously not of itself sufficient to understand the capacity for willing, for the subject must also be capable of affirming or rejecting those desires. Fichte elaborates upon the form that this "absolute" capacity of the practical subject assumes in his claim that "the absolute nature of real action . . . comes under the *jurisdiction of the concept* and only then becomes genuine *freedom.*"[21] The kind of concept Fichte has in mind here is what he calls a *Zweckbegriff,* or "purposive concept." Thus, to say that the "absoluteness" of the practical subject "comes under the jurisdiction of concepts" must be to claim that the will's transition from its original indeterminacy to a determined state (i.e., to willing a particular something) takes place in accord with the subject's conception of the purpose it wants to pursue through its action. The subject's choice between two or more courses of action, though not caused by something external to itself, is not therefore simply undetermined, but is grounded instead upon a conception of one's goal, which serves as the standard for choosing among the available options. Furthermore, it is only when such a purposive concept is involved in the will's determination of itself that its action is *genuinely* free, as opposed to merely uncaused, or undetermined. Fichte's statement that the will's *Unbestimmbarkeit* becomes freedom only when it is subjected to the rule of concepts is to be taken as a rejection of the idea that the subject somehow exists originally as free and that, in addition to this quality, it also possesses the capacity to exercise its freedom in a rational way (i.e., in accord with concepts). Fichte's view, rather, must be that the subject's freedom, its ability to resist the impulses of nature and to determine itself in any meaningful sense, depends upon, and is inseparable from, its existence as an intelligence (*Intelligenz*), as a being that is capable of constructing and employing concepts. True willing involves, then, the ability not only to abstract from one's present desires, but also to choose one's determining incentives on the basis of a concept or, in other words, for a subjective reason.

In the following passage Fichte elaborates upon the role played by *Zweckbegriffe* in free willing:

abstraction from everything that one values. On the contrary, it is precisely on the basis of these value commitments that one's immediate desires are to be judged.

21. "Jene Absolutheit des reellen Handelns . . . kommt unter die *Botmäßigkeit des Begriffs;* und dadurch erst wird sie eigentliche *Freiheit*" (SW, IV, p. 32).

The free being determines itself only with and according to concepts. Thus, its choice must be grounded upon a concept relating
to the choice, to that which is to be chosen. Let us say that a choice
is to be made among *A*, *B* and *C*. If the free being chooses one of
them – for example, *C* – can it prefer *C* without any ground whatsoever, that is, without an intelligible ground in a concept? Absolutely not, for then the choice would not take place through
freedom but rather through blind chance. Freedom acts in accord
with concepts. There must be something in *C* by virtue of which it
becomes preferable. Let us call this something *X*. . . . How does it
happen, then, that *X* determines the choice rather than some possible not-*X*? This can only have its ground in a general rule that the
rational being already possesses, . . . which Kant . . . calls a
maxim.[22]

While this passage contains a clear statement of the role of purposive concepts in willing, it also complicates Fichte's account
somewhat by introducing the further notion of a maxim. Although
Fichte distinguishes here between a *Zweckbegriff* and a maxim, he
clearly understands the two to be intimately related and equally
essential to a freely willed act. Let us try to make Fichte's example
here more concrete: I choose *C* (a run in the park) over *B* (a nap
in the sun) on the basis of some general feature of the former (*X*)
that distinguishes *C* from its rival *B*. It is this general feature *X*
that Fichte apparently refers to by the term *Zweckbegriff*, and this
is to be taken to indicate simply that my choice of *C* is made on the
basis of my conception of a particular purpose – in this case,
perhaps the enjoyment afforded by physical exercise or, alternatively, the state of good health it helps me to maintain.

Fichte's additional point is that the adoption of a particular
Zweckbegriff is itself grounded in a general rule, or maxim, that
ranks one purpose over another. The choice described here could
conceivably be based upon a number of distinct maxims, but let
us consider only two possibilities: In the less complicated case
I simply enjoy jogging more than sunbathing and thus choose
to do the former. Here the maxim that governs my action is merely
a subjective preference for *C* over *B*, and the kind of "reflection"
involved in this choice consists in nothing more than consulting my preferences. In a second case I find running tedious, and
my immediate impulse is to lie in the sun instead. However, in

22. SW, IV, p. 179.

reflecting upon that desire and the alternative available to me, I realize that exercise will be of greater benefit to my health and choose it for that reason. Here my reflection upon my immediate desire is somewhat more complicated, as is mirrored in the fact that my act is determined by a higher-level maxim that ranks that which is necessary for good health as preferable to passive amusement.

Although this sketch leaves certain questions unanswered as to the role played by maxims in formal self-determination,[23] let us turn now to a more general question about Fichte's account, namely, Why should we regard a choice grounded in a *Zweckbegriff* and maxim as free, or self-determined? At least two distinct answers are suggested by Fichte's text. In the passage quoted earlier Fichte characterizes free action as following from a maxim that the subject "already possesses." The conclusion one might draw from this is that merely to determine my actions in accord with a general rule represents itself a significant, though perhaps not the deepest, form of self-determination, regardless of the origin of that rule – that is, regardless of whether the rule itself is in some fundamental way "self-given." Fichte's more characteristic position, however, is that the maxims that govern even the subject's formally free choices are themselves freely chosen, or given by the subject to itself "by means of absolute spontaneity,"[24] as opposed to having their origin in something external to the will: A maxim "becomes a maxim through an act of my own freedom, [that is,] . . . by means of the fact that I, as empirical subject, freely make it into a rule for my action."[25] Thus, Fichte's view seems to be that, although one always chooses to act on the basis of some reason, what one allows to count as a decisive reason must depend, at least in part, upon the subject's spontaneity. Moreover, Fichte seems to hold the position that if this spontaneity were not involved in the adoption of maxims, "all freedom would be nullified."[26]

Thus, there seem to be two possible ways of understanding the status of the subject's determining maxims in Fichte's account of

---

23. For example, to what extent must the subject be conscious of its determining maxims in order for its actions to be regarded as free? We shall return to this question later in the discussion of "full" formal freedom. The upshot of Fichte's apparent position is that the subject is capable of various degrees of awareness of its maxims and that the more one is explicitly aware of them prior to acting, the freer the action. On this view, then, the freedom of *Willkür* would be subject to differences of degree. See SW, IV, pp. 153–4, 198.
24. SW, IV, p. 181. See also p. 198.   25. SW, IV, p. 180.
26. "So würde alle übrige Freiheit aufgehoben" (SW, IV, p. 180).

formal self-determination. On one interpretation, the origin of a maxim is irrelevant to the issue of whether the act that proceeds from it is to be regarded as formally free. Any act that is done for a reason, as opposed to having a cause in nature, is to be considered to have been freely willed. Furthermore, it is not implausible to regard this notion of freedom as a species of self-determination, since my particular acts are determined in accord with a principle that, in a very straightforward sense, is "my own." The second interpretation (and the one that seems to have been Fichte's dominant position) holds that an act is free only when its determining maxim is itself a product of the subject's own spontaneity. On this view the practical subject's determining power (the "absoluteness" of its will) ultimately resides in its capacity to determine freely which maxims will govern its actions, a capacity that is characterized here simply as a kind of spontaneity. I shall not try to resolve this ambiguity in Fichte's position, for I believe that it is ultimately irrelevant to an understanding of the larger aims of the *Sittenlehre* and its analysis of self-determination in its more substantive form. The reason for this is that, on Fichte's view, *neither* of the two cases distinguished here succeeds at comprehending self-determination in the deepest sense of the term. This is because neither position offers an account of the subject's adoption of maxims that allows for those maxims to be understood as "its own" in a sufficiently substantive sense. This is obvious in the first case, where one's maxims might well have their source in something external to the subject, but there is an important sense in which it is true of the second scenario as well. For in Fichte's elaboration of the latter view, nothing more is said about the subject's adoption of maxims apart from an appeal to its spontaneity. If the account of self-determination were to end here, then the subject could be held to determine itself through rational reflection with respect to its particular actions, but with respect to its maxims it would be self-determined only in the most abstract of senses. For merely to say that the subject adopts or rejects its maxims spontaneously is to leave open the possibility that its spontaneity consists in nothing more than arbitrary choice. But if this were so, in what sense would the subject's maxims really be "its own"? In what significant sense would they be *self*-determined? In the absence of a more developed account of the subject's spontaneity, the difference between the two views sketched here is of less consequence than initially seemed to be the case. It is precisely this line of thought, I believe, that informs Fichte's main project in the *Sittenlehre*. This general view finds its expression in the fact that Fichte calls the kind of freedom analyzed above "formal freedom." To call this species of freedom "formal" is not to deny that it is genuinely freedom – it is even properly considered a kind of "self-determination"[27] – but only to indicate that it should not be taken to represent self-determination in its fullest sense.

This point invites us to ask how Fichte in fact conceives of substantive self-determination. Our discussion of the limits of the merely formal freedom involved in all willing constitutes a good first step toward an answer to this question, for it suggests a way of formulating more precisely what such an account should attempt to explain. The principal task faced by Fichte's theory of substantive self-determination can be understood as one of explaining how the practical subject can be self-determining, not only on the level of its particular actions, but also with respect to the maxims that guide those deeds. In other words, is it possible to conceive of the subject as capable of giving its maxims to itself "spontaneously" in such a way that its espousal of maxims is more than merely arbitrary? Fichte's answer to this question in its most general form will be that the subject can be self-determining with respect to its maxims only by virtue of a particular relation that it establishes to itself. This very abstract characterization of Fichte's position is fairly easy to glean from his texts. The real difficulty consists in articulating more precisely the nature of this crucial self-relation and in understanding how it enables one to comprehend the possibility of substantive self-determination. An attempt to carry out this task brings us back to a question alluded to earlier concerning the relevance of Fichte's analysis of willing in general at the beginning of the *Sittenlehre* to his treatment of the more important issue of substantive self-determination. We have already seen one way in which the earlier account is relevant here: An examination of formal self-determination enabled us to see more clearly what a theory of substantive self-determination should attempt to accomplish. But for Fichte the discussion of formal freedom plays a more essential role than this. As we shall see,

27. Recall Fichte's statement, cited earlier, that all willing involves a "determining of oneself by oneself" (SW, IV, p. 22). Kant, too, uses 'self-determination' to refer to this notion of freedom, as evidenced by the passage from KRV, A534/B562, quoted earlier.

the most common way in which he characterizes the self-relation that is fundamental to substantive self-determination is in terms of the subject's reflection upon its own capacity for willing – or, what is the same, upon its formal freedom.

Substantive self-determination

The universalist account

We have already seen that, on Fichte's view, the main goal of an account of substantive self-determination is to explain how the subject can determine its own practical maxims, not in a merely arbitrary manner, but in accord with "norms" that it somehow gives to itself. Before examining Fichte's attempts to explain how this is possible, we must say something more about the notion of a norm that is involved in substantive self-determination. It is not surprising, given his Kantian heritage, that Fichte sometimes characterizes his strong notion of self-determination as a kind of autonomy, or "self-legislation" (*Selbstgesetzgebung*). Since autonomy consists in the giving of laws to oneself, it seems reasonable to look to Fichte's notion of a practical "law" to provide us with a conception of the kind of norms required for substantive self-determination.[28]

Although Fichte never provides an adequately detailed analysis of this crucial concept, he does at one point characterize a law as the "inviolable maxim of all of [one's] willing."[29] This definition, terse as it is, makes reference to two important characteristics of a practical law: First, a law is itself a kind of maxim and, second, since it governs "all of one's willing," it is universal and therefore a maxim of the most general sort. What this seems to mean for Fichte is that a practical law expresses the subject's "highest"

28. Our concern here is to articulate in a more general way than Fichte himself does the minimal conditions that must be satisfied in order for a higher-level maxim to be considered a "norm" and hence capable of having a role in substantive self-determination. Fichte's notion of a practical law is regarded here as one example of a norm that would satisfy these conditions. As such, it can provide us with a closer conception of the general features a norm must have, but since the notion of law is bound up with only one of his accounts of substantive self-determination (i.e., the one closest to Kant's theory of moral autonomy), it should not be regarded as the only possible exemplification of a norm for self-determination in the stronger sense.

29. SW, IV, p. 56.

maxim, a principle of action that, though not necessarily *determining* every particular deed, is never *violated* in one's willing. As such, a law must be understood as a kind of higher-order maxim capable of ranking and harmonizing other possible maxims.[30] Hence, a law can be conceived of as articulating a subject's highest value, which establishes a kind of consistency among its actions and maxims. The consistency provided by such a practical law, however, does not by itself constitute autonomy for Fichte. Self-determination in a substantive sense requires more than merely the circumstance that there exist a highest principle to order one's maxims; that principle must also in some sense be given to the subject by itself.

But what can it mean to give practical principles to oneself? In the first place, there is an important restriction upon the *content* of those principles that can play a role in substantive self-determination. One way of formulating this restriction is to say that such principles must be "norms," but this is of little help unless we specify how norms differ from other, "nonnormative" maxims. Thus far we have characterized norms only as higher-order maxims capable of determining an agent's lower-level maxims. Yet clearly Fichte does not consider *all* higher-level maxims to be possible norms for substantive self-determination. The fact that the latter is to involve *self-given* norms means that there is a class of higher-order maxims that, because they can never be self-given in a significant sense, cannot be considered potential maxims for substantive self-determination. In order for a norm to count as "self-given," it must (minimally) be more than what might be called a "maxim of nature" (a maxim the agent possesses solely by virtue of her existence as a being subject to natural desires). The kinds of higher-order maxims that Fichte wants to rule out here are those that are based solely upon the maximization of natural pleasure.[31] It is obvious that such a principle is capable of functioning as a higher-order maxim for determining lower-level maxims. The case described earlier of my choosing to jog even though

---

30. Even though a "highest" maxim ranks and harmonizes other, lower-level maxims, it need not be capable of resolving every possible conflict between lower-level principles. This is true, for example, in Kant's moral theory, where the supreme law, the categorical imperative, is incapable of deciding between two conflicting maxims of happiness if each has the same moral worth.

31. This is Fichte's point at SW, IV, p. 180, where he associates the "natural drive" (*Naturtrieb*) with the maxim of choosing whatever "promises the greatest pleasure with respect to intensity and duration."

I prefer a nap in the sun is an example of such maximization of pleasure, if, for example, the choice is made for the reason that the long-term pleasure afforded by good health is judged to outweigh the momentary displeasure of vigorous exercise. On this scenario, the decision to run could not qualify as an instance of substantive self-determination. For even though it involves the evaluation of low-level maxims by higher ones, the maxim upon which the choice is ultimately based expresses a purely "natural" purpose.[32] But if self-given norms may not be "natural" maxims, what kind of maxims will they be? One obvious response is suggested by Kant's distinction between natural and *moral* purposes, but there is no reason that all nonnatural norms must be moral in a strictly Kantian sense. Also to be included here are any principles of value that are not based upon a mere calculation of homogeneous pleasures and pains but that evaluate desires in qualitative rather than purely quantitative terms.[33]

Given that only certain higher-order maxims can be regarded as norms, we still need to consider the further question of how norms can be given to the subject by itself. We can begin to answer this question by returning to Fichte's notion of a practical law and asking what it means to give such a law to oneself. There is one sense in which the existence of any practical law requires the active participation of the subject, for presumably the consistency of will that is secured by such a law does not ever arise naturally, that is, without the subject's commitment to make a particular maxim an inviolable principle for its willing.[34] Yet the notion of self-determination that Fichte wants to articulate requires more than this. It is not sufficient that the subject commit itself to following any general principle whatsoever; that principle must be "its own" in a deeper sense. One way of formulating this extra requirement is to say that the *content* of the highest maxim must

32. This same point is made in Charles Taylor's consideration of a man who postpones the satisfaction of his immediate hunger in order to swim first and eat later on the grounds that doing so maximizes his pleasure, since the enjoyment of swimming and eating outweighs that of eating alone. See Taylor (1983, p. 113). A longer version of the essay appears as "What Is Human Agency?" (1985).

33. For example, the judgment that one desire is higher or lower, more worthy or less worthy, more or less noble than another. Hence, the concept of a norm articulated here corresponds roughly to Taylor's notion of "strong evaluation" (1983, pp. 112–17).

34. This, I take it, is part of Fichte's point at SW, IV, p. 56, where he articulates different senses in which a law can be given by the subject to itself.

also be given to the subject by itself.[35] In attempting to explain how such self-legislation is possible Fichte refers again to his earlier notion of a *Zweckbegriff*. Since a practical law consists in a subject's most general maxim, it can be regarded as an expression of what one values most highly or, alternatively, of how one conceives of one's "highest purpose" (*Endzweck*).[36] To give oneself a law, then, is to embrace a particular *Zweckbegriff* as supreme over all others, as embodying the most important purpose to be pursued in one's life. In order to be autonomous in the deepest sense, however, the supreme *Zweckbegriff* that is adopted must be "constructed by myself." Thus, the task of explaining how a practical law can be self-given becomes one of characterizing how the subject constructs for itself a concept of its highest purpose. In carrying out this task Fichte's primary concern is not to specify *which* purposive concept the subject must adopt as its highest in order to be truly self-determined. What he focuses upon, rather, is *how* the subject comes to construct such a concept for itself. Put in another way, Fichte regards his main task as consisting not in spelling out which norms the autonomous agent ought to have but in answering the question: What does it mean for a subject to adopt its norms in a self-determined mode? More specifically, in what kind of relation to itself must the self-determining subject stand?[37]

A hint at Fichte's conception of the self-relation that is essential to substantive self-determination is given in a statement that

35. This is the point implicit in Fichte's oft-repeated claim (considered later) that my highest *Zweckbegriff* must be "constructed by myself" (*von mir selbst entworfen*), that it must be my "own product" (SW, IV, p. 155). To say that the content of the law (not of the lower-level maxims) must be given by the subject to itself does not exclude the possibility that the law might be of an extremely formal nature, such as Kant's categorical imperative. 'Content' here refers to "what the law commands." In Kant's case, although the moral law does not command any particular maxims, it does have a content in the sense that it requires all lower-level maxims to meet the formal condition of universalizability.

36. The concept of a "highest purpose," like the notion of a law's "content" discussed earlier, is intended in a very general sense such that even Kant's purely formal notion of autonomy could be considered a kind of *Endzweck*. For Kant my *Endzweck* would consist in willing only those maxims that can be universalized.

37. This characterization of Fichte's aim is consistent with Tugendhat's observation that "it is only since Fichte and Kierkegaard that it has seemed necessary to relate the question of the right mode of conduct not only to normative contents but also to the way in which I appropriate them for myself as an individual, that is, to the way in which I relate to myself in their appropriation." See Tugendhat (1986, p. 131).

appears throughout the *Sittenlehre* in a number of formulations: "By means of its absolute reflection upon itself, the subject tears itself away from everything external to itself, gains control over itself and makes itself absolutely self-sufficient."[38] This statement makes clear that Fichte intends to locate the subject's capacity to determine itself in its ability to step back from its given nature (i.e., from its drives and desires) and to reflect upon itself and its situation. This general idea is already familiar to us from Fichte's analysis of willing in general, for formal self-determination was seen there to require a kind of reflection as well. In that earlier case the subject was described as reflecting upon itself as a *Natur-wesen* – that is, as a being that finds itself motivated by a variety of natural incentives – and then choosing among those incentives on the basis of a particular purposive concept. It should be clear, however, that an account of substantive self-determination requires something more, for what we are attempting to understand in this case is not merely the capacity for free choice but the subject's ability to construct for itself a conception of its highest purpose. Whereas formal self-determination is consistent with the subject's free adoption of any purpose whatsoever, substantive self-determination requires the subject to will in accord with a specific kind of *Zweckbegriff*, one that embodies the subject's supreme value and that it "gives to itself." It is for this reason that when characterizing substantive self-determination Fichte further specifies the notion of reflection referred to earlier as "the subject's absolutely free reflection upon itself *in its true essential nature (in seinem wahren Wesen)*."[39] Thus, choosing in a fully self-determined mode requires that I reflect upon "my true nature" and make choices that are in accord with that nature, choices that are in some sense expressions of "who I really am." In other words, in substantive self-determination this conception of "who I am essentially" is to serve as the "norm in accord with which [the subject is to] determine itself freely."[40] This general formulation seems plausible enough, but it raises two crucial questions: What is contained in Fichte's notion of a subject's essential nature? And,

---

38. This statement occurs nowhere in the *Sittenlehre* in precisely this form, but it is a translation of a passage at SW, IV, p. 133, with some interpolations (in brackets) from SW, IV, p. 73: "Durch die [absolute] Reflexion [auf sich selbst] reißt das Ich sich los von allem, was außer ihm sein soll, bekommt sich selbst in seine eigene Gewalt und stellt sich absolut selbständig hin."
39. SW, IV, p. 57, my emphasis.   40. SW, IV, p. 52.

once its content is specified, how can this notion function as a normative guide for one's actions? Since neither of these questions can be answered in a straightforward way, we shall restrict ourselves for the present to a consideration of the first.

Unfortunately, the *Sittenlehre* does not provide us with a clear answer to even this most basic of questions. In fact, the text suggests that Fichte unwittingly embraced two different answers to this question, each of which implies a distinct conception of self-determination. The distinction between the two answers is best characterized as follows: When I reflect upon my "true nature," am I supposed to consider "who I really am" as *me,* this particular individual, or am I to reflect upon some universal feature of my identity, for example, who I am *qua* rational subject? Fichte's actual discussion of substantive self-determination fails to distinguish consistently between these two questions and, as one would expect, winds up following paths that lead in two different directions. The second alternative, which we shall examine first, is the more prominent in the *Sittenlehre,* and, beyond this, it shares deep affinities, at least in intention, with Kant's own attempt to deduce moral obligation from a universal feature of the human subject, namely, its capacity for rationality. Let us call this account Fichte's "universalist" conception of substantive self-determination. This account is intended to articulate a notion of self-determination that roughly corresponds to Kant's account of moral autonomy. Therefore, this version of Fichte's project is most consistent with his long-held goal of providing a firmer foundation for Kant's moral theory.

Yet, as I shall attempt to show, this account is beset by a number of confusions that make it considerably less interesting than one might initially think. For this reason we shall also examine a second notion of self-determination that derives from the first of the two alternatives. This account is admittedly less prominent in Fichte's writings, but it is present nonetheless, even though it remains undeveloped in important respects. As we shall see, this second account yields a notion of self-determination that is broader than Kant's purely moral conception of autonomy but that is still relevant to the practical question "How ought I to live my life?" We shall call this the "individualist" conception of substantive self-determination, since it understands the subject's "true nature" to refer to its nature as a particular individual. There are two reasons for paying so much attention to this second, undeveloped notion of self-determination: First, I believe that it is philosophically more interesting than the first of Fichte's conceptions; and, second, it is this interpretation that makes the most sense of Fichte's stated goal of understanding self-determination as dependent upon the "self-positing" that is unique to subjects.

Let us turn now to Fichte's universalist account of self-determination. As already mentioned, the principal way in which this view differs from the individualist conception is that it takes the question of the subject's "true nature" to refer to an essential feature of all subjects rather than to one's own individual nature. Fichte begins to develop this account by locating the essential feature of the subject that is relevant to self-determination in what he calls the I's "self-sufficiency" (*Selbständigkeit*): "The principle of morality is consciousness's necessary thought that it ought to determine its freedom in accord with the concept of self-sufficiency, unconditionally and without exception."[41] If it is my true nature as a subject to be self-sufficient, my actions are to be considered self-determined in the deepest sense when this conception of my nature functions as the *Zweckbegriff* that grounds them. In other words, my actions are self-determined when I choose them for the reason that they either further or are consistent with my nature as a self-sufficient being. The crucial concept here is clearly "self-sufficiency," but since this notion can be understood in a variety of ways, it is necessary to ask what precisely Fichte means by it. The term *Selbständigkeit* might also be translated as "independence," a notion that appears explicitly in Fichte's frequent characterizations of *Selbständigkeit* as "absolute independence from all of nature."[42] Yet what does it mean for a subject to be independent of nature? In the rare cases where Fichte addresses this issue explicitly, he resorts to a familiar notion: The I's self-sufficiency consists in its *Unbestimmbarkeit,* or its "absolute inability to be determined by anything external to the I."[43] Fichte's appeal to the I's *Unbestimmbarkeit* to explicate the notion of self-sufficiency makes it clear that he intends to use his earlier analysis of the radically undetermined, "absolute" nature of the will in all of its willing to provide him with a notion of the I's

---

41. SW, IV, p. 59. See also pp. 50–60 and throughout the work.
42. "Absolute Unabhängigkeit von aller Natur" (SW, IV, p. 131).
43. SW, IV, p. 56. Fichte also identifies the I's self-sufficiency with its freedom (p. 49), as well as with its *Absolutheit* (p. 50), a concept discussed earlier in conjunction with the notion of the absolute nature of all willing.

self-sufficiency that can serve as a norm for self-determined action in the strong sense. In other words, Fichte's suggestion seems to be that in reflecting upon my nature as a formally free being with the capacity to determine which of my incentives will govern my action, I attain a conception of myself as self-sufficient that can function as a standard for determining which actions among those available to me I ought to undertake. If some sense could be made of this scenario, then the actions chosen could be considered self-determined in the sense that they would follow from my "true nature" as a free, practical being.

This strategy ultimately fails for the simple reason that it is impossible to understand substantive self-determination merely in terms of the subject's reflection upon its capacity for formal freedom. In focusing upon the will's "independence from nature," what Fichte clearly has in mind is something akin to Kant's point that truly autonomous action requires one's will to be determined by a purely rational incentive, as opposed to one that derives from nature (i.e., sensuous desire). Thus, autonomy for Kant does involve an "independence from nature," but in a sense that is distinct from the way it is understood in Fichte's original account of willing. According to the latter, the practical subject is independent from nature in all of its willing in the sense that an incentive, of whatever kind, cannot determine the will on its own. This is true not only when duty is opposed to desire but also when natural desires conflict. In this sense I am independent from nature *whenever* I will, regardless of the content of my choices. Since it is taken as a fact that the human will is independent from nature in this sense, it is difficult to see how reflection upon this feature of the practical subject could give rise to norms for self-determined action. Surely no amount of reflection upon the mere fact of my capacity for free choice can help me to decide which course of action I ought to follow.

In addition to this suggestion that reflection upon my formal freedom can provide me with my highest *Zweckbegriff,* Fichte alludes to a weaker sense in which reflection upon one's "inability to be determined by nature" (*Unbestimmbarkeit durch die Natur*) could be said to play a role in self-determination:

> When I become aware of my merely formal freedom, I . . . thereby acquire the capacity to postpone the [immediate] satisfaction of nature, . . . and at the same time I acquire the capacity to reflect

upon the natural drive in the different forms in which it offers itself to me and *to choose among the various possible satisfactions of it.* . . . I choose with full freedom of the will (*mit völliger Willensfreiheit*), for I choose with a consciousness of [my] self-determination.[44]

The crux of Fichte's claim here apparently is that to be explicitly aware of my formal freedom prior to acting has the effect of deepening the sense in which I am free. What Fichte has in mind must be the following: To be expressly aware of the fact that I am capable of free choice is to realize that what I do depends ultimately upon me rather than upon forces outside of my control. This realization itself, however, can move me to reflect more carefully upon the choice before me in order to determine which of the alternatives I want to pursue. This interpretation of Fichte's notion of the "full freedom of the will" is consistent with his further characterizations of it as "acting with circumspection (*Besonnenheit*) and consciousness" and as "being conscious of the reason (*Grund*) for which I act as I do."[45] This "full" freedom is contrasted with "finding the rule in accord with which the act . . . occurred only after the fact."[46] Thus, the distinction made here between "full" freedom and a state that is somehow less free turns upon the difference between consciously followed maxims and maxims that determine actions more or less unconsciously. This implies that the extent to which one is fully free depends upon the degree to which one is explicitly aware of the rules that in fact govern one's actions. Hence, this distinction does not coincide with the one made between substantive and formal self-determination, but rather operates within the sphere of formal freedom itself: Some of our formally free actions are fully free in the sense that the reasons for which they are done are explicitly known by the agent prior to action, while others – those in which the determining maxims remain partly obscure to the agent – must be considered less free. Nevertheless, if "full freedom of the will" in this sense does not yet *constitute* substantive self-determination, it is certainly not irrelevant to it, and indeed, may plausibly be regarded as a necessary condition for it. For if true self-determination consists in the subject's capacity to evaluate its own maxims in relation to a highest, self-given principle and to determine its particular actions in accord with this evaluation, then the subject must be capable both

44. SW, IV, pp. 161–2.   45. SW, IV, p. 154.   46. SW, IV, p. 188.

of knowing the real reasons behind its actions and of engaging in a substantial degree of reflective deliberation prior to acting.

Fichte's inability to account for substantive self-determination in terms of the subject's reflection upon its self-sufficiency (where 'self-sufficiency' is understood as the subject's freedom from determination by nature) should lead us to ask whether there might not be another way of interpreting the I's "independence from nature" that could make Fichte's account somewhat more plausible. There is, in fact, a second and very different sense that Fichte sometimes gives to the notion of self-sufficiency, but unfortunately, as we shall see, it too proves incapable of serving as the basis for an adequate account of self-determination in the desired sense. This second sense of self-sufficiency is especially prominent in later passages of the *Sittenlehre*, where "our complete independence from everything external to us" is clearly meant to refer not to a subjective aspect of agency but to "an objective state" (*einen objektiven Zustand*) that one's actions bring about. Hence, this strand of Fichte's thought defines the subject's self-sufficiency in terms of its relation to an objective set of circumstances produced by its own action. To qualify as "self-determined" in this sense, an action must foster my objective freedom from nature; it must be "part of a series which, if continued, would have to lead to the I's independence."[47] According to this view, a subject is self-determined when "the intention, the concept of its acting, aims at complete liberation from nature"[48] or, in other words, when the highest *Zweckbegriff* in accord with which it orders all other maxims embodies the aim of freeing itself from the objective constraints of nature.

What does it mean, though, for the subject to have an objective existence in which it is free from nature? Once again, Fichte understands this idea in a number of ways. In the first place, the notion of the I's independence from nature is reminiscent of his position in the WL 1794 that the I's essential nature resides in its striving to eliminate limits imposed upon it by the not-I. As we saw, this idea had there a primarily moral content, according to which it was the I's essential *Bestimmung*, or vocation, to realize moral purposes within the empirical world. This was understood not only as a demand that moral intentions be translated into real actions but, more significantly, as urging that the objective world itself be rearranged so as to foster the moral development of the agents who inhabit it. This strictly moral interpretation of the subject's objective "independence from nature" is still present in the *Sittenlehre*, but it is no longer the only, or even the predominant, sense Fichte gives to the notion. For in many places he seems to have in mind simply a naturalistic ideal in which the human species attains a state of complete domination over nature in the sense that we learn successfully to realize all human purposes within the world, including those that derive from our sensuous nature alone.[49] At still other times Fichte defines self-sufficiency as the individual's appropriation of the powers of nature, his ability to make the natural world a mere extension of himself, as an instrument of his particular will:

> Self-sufficiency, our ultimate goal, consists . . . in that state of affairs in which everything is dependent upon me and I am not dependent upon anything, where everything that I will occurs in my sensible world simply because I will it to be so, just as in the case of my body, the starting point of my absolute causality. The world must become for me what my body is for me. Now, to be sure, this goal is unattainable, but nevertheless I should always advance towards it – that is, I should work upon (*bearbeiten*) everything in the sensible world so that it comes to be a means for the attainment of this final purpose.[50]

Taken at face value, the notion that our highest ethical goal consists in making the world into a corporeal extension of our will surely counts as one of Fichte's more outrageous ideas. Yet what underlies this, as well as his various other conceptions of self-sufficiency as an "objective state," is the more serious claim that self-determination in its deepest form is not a wholly subjective affair but one that requires some kind of expression in the objec-

---

49. This aspect is especially prominent in Fichte's popular writings. See, e.g., his impassioned description of the future in Fichte (1956, pp. 102–4; SW, II, pp. 266–9): "Cultivation shall quicken and ameliorate the sluggish and baleful atmosphere of primeval forests, deserts and marshes. . . . Nature shall become more and more intelligible and transparent; . . . human power . . . shall rule over her without difficulty, and the conquest, once made, shall be peacefully maintained." And so on.
50. SW, IV, p. 229.

tive world as well. While Fichte's scattered remarks on this topic are philosophically provocative (as evidenced by their influence on later German philosophy), they nevertheless fall far short of constituting a coherent and adequately elaborated conception of the subject's *Selbständigkeit* as an objective state of freedom from nature.

Apart from this objection, there is another problem with defining substantive self-determination in terms of an objective state that is more relevant to our purposes here. Even if we grant Fichte's intuition that true self-determination requires some kind of realization in the external world, something more substantial is needed for a complete account of self-determination. The problem with this strategy as Fichte executes it is that it defines the subject's autonomy only in terms of its independence from something – in this case, something that is conceived as radically "other" – without being able to say more positively what self-determination is. If it means anything at all, "independence from nature" must refer to the subject's ability to accomplish its own purposes unhindered by natural impediments. But then the main question of a theory of self-determination remains unanswered: What does it mean for a subject to have "its own" purposes? It is certainly possible to conceive of these purposes in wholly naturalistic terms as the totality of natural needs characteristic of an embodied subject. Although Fichte does not completely disregard these purely natural purposes, it is clearly not his intention simply to identify a subject's self-given purposes with the promptings of nature. In the absence of any further analysis of what it means for the practical subject to determine its own goals, an account of substantive self-determination as mere independence from nature remains rather empty: The subject strives to free itself from nature in order to realize its own purposes, but how, and from where, does it obtain these purposes that are allegedly its own? It is precisely this question that Fichte's account is intended to answer.

This marks the end of our examination of the first group of Fichte's attempts to construct a theory of substantive self-determination. As I outlined earlier, what the members of this group have in common is the view that self-determination consists in the subject's determination of its actions in accord with its "essential nature," where that notion is taken to refer to an essential, universal feature of subjects in general. The main conclusion to be drawn from the foregoing analysis is that the central notion behind these conceptions – that the I's *Selbständigkeit* constitutes its essential nature – is represented by Fichte in such a variety of ways that it is difficult to reconstruct a single, coherent account of how substantive self-determination is to be understood. Moreover, none of the alternatives sketched thus far seems a very promising first step toward an account that could explain what it means for a subject to give itself general practical principles.

In what follows I shall try to show that Fichte's second way of conceiving of substantive self-determination – what I referred to earlier as his "individualist" conception – is more interesting than the first, despite the fact that it is found in the *Sittenlehre* only in an undeveloped form. Before turning to this task, however, let us briefly note two points concerning the relationship between these alternative conceptions. First, and most important, the two accounts employ fundamentally distinct notions of substantive self-determination. Although both understand self-determination to be willing in accord with one's "true nature," the second takes one's "nature" to refer not to an essential feature of *all* subjects but to the different natures of particular individuals. Second, Fichte does not address the issue of whether there are significant connections between these notions of self-determination. The two are simply presented side by side in his texts and appear to be developed in complete independence of each other. The most likely explanation for his failure to integrate the two accounts is that, as is so often the case with Fichte, he himself was unaware of the different strands within his own position. As we shall see later, one important consequence of this fact is that Fichte was unable to develop the basic idea underlying this second conception into a fully articulated theory of substantive self-determination.

The individualist account

We shall begin this account of self-determination by demonstrating that Fichte does indeed sometimes conceive of the subject's "true nature" in terms of an individual's particular nature, or "character," rather than as a universal essence of subjects per se. As we saw at the beginning of this chapter, Fichte understands the task of his account of substantive self-determination to consist in explaining in what sense the practical subject can be "its own ground," and one of the ways in which he conceives of this self-groundedness is as the subject's ability to make itself into the kind of individual it wants to be: "Originally, i.e., apart from its own doing, the subject *is* absolutely nothing: what it is to *become*, it must make itself into by means of its own activity."[51] That Fichte has in mind here the different natures of particular individuals is made clear by passages such as the following:

> Who am I really – that is, what kind of an individual am I? And what is the reason that I am *that* individual? I answer: I am . . . *that individual into whom I freely make myself, and I am this* [kind of individual] *because I make myself into it.*[52]

What Fichte is alluding to here is clearly some notion of *individual* character,[53] which includes the idea that one's nature is in some sense self-created rather than merely given. The notion of a self-created character, as well as the attempt to relate this notion to the topic of self-determination, are not themes unique to Fichte but have their origin, I would suggest, in a particular part of Kant's moral philosophy, namely, his theory of moral disposition (*Gesinnung*) and its relation to free choice, or *Willkür*. Before considering Fichte's account, it will be helpful to examine in some detail Kant's own understanding of moral disposition, especially insofar as it is a response to a particular conception of *Willkür* that is found in Reinhold's moral theory. Since the version of Fichte's account of self-determination under consideration here can be seen as a part of this very debate, our treatment of Kant and Reinhold will be less a detour than a first step toward understanding Fichte's view.

Fichte's interest in the notion of *Willkür* and its relation to moral theory does not originate in 1798 with the publication of the *Sittenlehre*. As early as 1793 Fichte was preoccupied with this issue,

---

51. SW, IV, p. 50; see also p. 38.
52. "Wer bin ich denn eigentlich, d.i. was für ein Individuum? Und welches ist der Grund, daß ich *der* bin? Ich antworte: ich bin . . . *derjenige, zu welchem ich mich mit Freiheit mache, und bin es darum, weil ich mich dazu mache*" (SW, IV, p. 222).
53. Tugendhat's interpretation supports this reading of Fichte's project as well: "Kant does not yet mean by autonomy a self-determination of the person as a person or of the I as an I, but a self-determination of reason. It is Fichte who first attempts to understand the rationality of the person on the basis of the I's relation to itself" (Tugendhat, pp. 133–4; translation amended).

as evidenced by the Creuzer review,[54] which is devoted almost exclusively to the task of giving a coherent account of the kind of freedom characteristic of *Willkür*. In this early text Fichte argues that it is essential to distinguish between two senses of freedom – or, in his words, between two kinds of "absolute self-activity" (*absolute Selbsttätigkeit*) – both of which are required by Kant's moral philosophy. The first kind of "self-activity" is that "by means of which reason is practical and gives itself a law."[55] Although Fichte does not elaborate upon this conception in the Creuzer review, it is clear that this sense of self-activity corresponds to the most prominent notion of freedom in Kant's moral theory, namely, the idea of moral autonomy, which is defined as determining one's will in accord with self-prescribed laws of reason, independently of desire and natural inclination. In choosing to follow the moral law the subject is autonomous because it stands under no laws other than those that it gives to itself. Under this conception, freedom is coextensive with morality. To act immorally – or amorally – is to act in accord with "external" incentives that are given to the subject by nature. This stands in contrast to true self-determination through the adoption of incentives supplied to oneself by the faculty of reason.

For the present it is unnecessary to explore this conception of autonomy in greater detail, since it is the second notion of freedom that is of greater concern to us here. The latter is defined by Fichte as "that by means of which the human being determines himself (in this function, his *will*) to obey or disobey [the moral] law."[56] Although every human being, by virtue of being rational, stands under the obligation to follow the moral law, not every individual in fact chooses the path of moral action. It is this aspect of freedom – the individual's choice to follow or to disregard the dictates of the moral law – that is involved in the second sense of freedom. This act of choice is a kind of freedom, because presumably it is carried out by the will alone, independently of anything external to itself. The will either accepts or rejects the moral law as determining its own maxim, and this choice cannot be explained or predicted on the basis of factors outside of the will itself.

54. This article is Fichte's review of Leonhard Creuzer's book *Skeptische Betrachtungen über die Freiheit des Willens mit Hinsicht auf die neuesten Theorien über dieselben* (GA, I.2, pp. 7–14; SW, VIII, pp. 411–17).
55. SW, VIII, p. 412.   56. SW, VIII, p. 412.

It should be obvious that the two senses of freedom distinguished here by Fichte are intended to correspond to the distinction between the will (*Wille*) and the faculty of choice (*Willkür*), which was articulated by Kant in its most explicit form in 1793, after the publication of the second *Critique*, in his work entitled *Religion Within the Bounds of Reason Alone*.[57] That Kant considers *Willkür* to involve a kind of freedom is evidenced by his frequent use of the locution "freedom of choice" (*Freiheit der Willkür*). Furthermore, it is clear that this sense of freedom is intended not to replace the notion of freedom as moral autonomy but to represent a species of freedom that is distinct from that of autonomy, and yet equally essential to a full account of morality. It is not difficult to see why this second sense of freedom is required by Kant's moral theory. As long as the only sense of freedom available to Kant is defined in terms of the autonomy involved in following the moral law, then all nonmoral acts must be regarded as unfree. The problematic implication of this view is that immoral actions would then not be free, and therefore one could not ascribe moral responsibility to the individuals who commit them. If, however, the notion of the freedom of choice is incorporated into the theory, then immoral acts can still be considered unfree in the deepest sense (i.e., in that they are not autonomous), but they can nevertheless be regarded as freely chosen and, for that reason, their agents may be held morally responsible for them.

As mentioned earlier, one of the concerns that plagued Fichte

---

57. Henceforth cited as *Religion*. English translation by Theodore M. Greene and Hoyt H. Hudson (1960); original in *Akademie-Ausgabe*, VI. It is unclear to what degree this distinction is already present within Kant's earlier moral writings. It is sometimes suggested that Kant's distinction in the *Groundwork* between positive and negative freedom is a forerunner of the *Wille–Willkür* distinction. It seems to me, however, that the earlier version of the distinction is best understood not as articulating two distinct *kinds* of freedom but, rather, as two ways of conceptualizing the same thing. The negative conception of freedom is negative, not because it refers to a kind of freedom different from the positive sort, but because it merely defines freedom negatively, in terms of what it is not (i.e., natural causality), whereas the positive conception spells out more concretely what human freedom consists in (i.e., determination in accord with a self-given law). On the other hand, Kant's account of "practical freedom" in Canon I of the first *Critique* (A798–803/B826–31) is very close to his later conception of *Willkür*. What is clear is that Kant's explicit discussion of *Willkür* in the *Religion* is directly motivated by the criticism made by various contemporaries, including Reinhold, that Kant's moral theory required for its coherence some notion of the freedom of choice.

from the time of his earliest contact with Kant's moral philosophy was the question: What is the nature of *Willkür?* We have already examined Fichte's treatment of free choice in an earlier portion of this chapter. The notion of *Willkür* we are about to examine here has a somewhat narrower scope than that of free choice in general, for as Kant treats it in the *Religion, Willkür* has a purely *moral* significance, which means that what is at issue is not a choice between two morally equivalent actions but one between following the moral law and rejecting it. Nevertheless, this more specific treatment of *Willkür* is relevant to our earlier account as well, for Kant's notion of moral disposition can be seen as an attempt to give an answer to a question we encountered in Fichte's more general account of free choice: If free acts are grounded in subjective maxims, what, if anything, determines those maxims themselves? I want to argue that this same issue recurs in Fichte's attempt to give an account of substantive self-determination in the *Sittenlehre* and that the project undertaken there can be understood as an attempt to steer a middle course between two opposing ways of conceiving of *Willkür:* one as the capacity for carrying out isolated and arbitrary choices, the other as a faculty that is in some sense determined to choose in accord with one's fundamental, noumenal disposition. If we were to recast Fichte's dilemma in terms of the historical figures who hold these positions, we could characterize it as the choice between Reinhold's account of *Willkür* and the one offered by Kant.

Before the publication in 1792 of Kant's account of *Willkür* in Book I of the *Religion,* Reinhold developed his own account of *Willkür* in the second volume of his *Letters on Kantian Philosophy.*[58] There Reinhold adopts what is surely the most natural way to conceive of *Willkür,* namely, as the subject's ability to make spontaneous and completely undetermined choices from among the various practical possibilities it faces. Reinhold reasons that in order for the choices of *Willkür* to be free, they must be wholly spontaneous, which means for him that they must have no objective ground outside of the subject itself. This, for Reinhold, is equivalent to saying that these choices are not causally determined by some state of affairs external to the will. From this consideration Reinhold concludes that "the free act is nothing less

58. Reinhold (1792, II). See especially Letter 8.

than groundless (*grundlos*),"[59] or, as we might say, undetermined. This view of *Willkür* fits into the larger theory of moral agency in the following way: The practical subject is aware of itself as standing under a universal moral law that it gives to itself by virtue of its rational capacities. The practical nature of pure reason, then, consists in its ability to supply the subject with a general law that derives solely from its own rational nature without recourse to any empirically conditioned notions such as happiness. In addition to its awareness of the moral law, the rational subject is also able to feel respect for such a law, and this feeling is capable of serving as an incentive for choosing to follow the dictates of duty over the promptings of natural desire. But, since human beings are not only rational but sensually affected as well, other incentives in the form of natural inclinations will be pulling the will in opposing directions and competing with the moral incentive of respect to determine the will's course of action. In every instance of such moral conflict, the outcome, on Reinhold's view, is determined by an act of *Willkür*, an ungrounded and arbitrary choice between competing incentives.

Now it is clear that this notion of *Willkür* succeeds at solving the problem it was originally intended to address, for it enables one to ascribe freedom, and therefore merit or blame, to both moral and immoral deeds. Why, then, does Kant reject this account and formulate another in its stead? Rather than answer this question directly, let us turn first to Kant's alternative account of *Willkür* with the aim of contrasting the two positions in order to discover Kant's reasons for going beyond Reinhold's view. Since Kant's treatment of *Willkür* is considerably more complex than Reinhold's, we need to take a rather detailed look at Kant's account, especially in its most fully articulated form, in Book I of the *Religion*. Crucial to Kant's position here is the claim that all deeds in the sensible world are preceded, and determined by, a "subjective ground."[60] The term 'deed' here is significant, for it is certainly not Kant's view that all empirical *events* have a subjective

---

59. Reinhold (1792, II, p. 282).
60. *Religion*, p. 21; English, p. 16. In explicating the concept of human nature Kant refers to "the subjective ground of the use of one's freedom in general . . . , which precedes all sensible deeds" (*der subjektive Grund des Gebrauchs seiner Freiheit überhaupt . . . , der vor aller in die Sinne fallenden Tat vorhergeht*). Later references make clear though that the subjective ground does not precede its deed in a temporal sense.

ground, nor even that all of human behavior has such a ground. 'Deed', rather, refers to that class of human actions that we think of as resulting from the volitions of practical beings. What distinguishes these actions from other events, on Kant's view, is that they are to be explained on the basis of subjective rather than objective grounds. It is this notion of a subjective ground that accounts for the principal way in which Kant's account of *Willkür* diverges from Reinhold's, and this difference is based upon the following consideration: Both Kant and Reinhold agree that a necessary condition for *Willkür*'s choices to be free is that they be undetermined by an objective ground – or, what is the same, that they not be the causally determined effects of some objective process. On Kant's view, however, Reinhold errs in tacitly assuming that if a choice lacks an *objective* determining ground, it must then be completely groundless. Kant's strategy, in contrast, is to employ the notion of a *subjective* ground in order to explain the possibility of choice that is free but not therefore randomly chosen. Kant's view, in other words, is not that the free acts of *Willkür* are absolutely undetermined but rather that they are determined by grounds that have a subjective rather than objective nature.[61]

Now, how are we to conceive of a subjective ground that governs the exercise of freedom? The answer to this question is made explicit in the following passage from the *Religion:*

> The freedom of *Willkür* is of a wholly unique nature in that no incentive can determine *Willkür* to an action, except insofar as the human being has incorporated that incentive into its maxim (has made it into a general rule in accord with which he will conduct himself).[62]

In part, this passage simply makes the general point that the freedom characteristic of *Willkür* consists in the fact that mere incentives never of themselves determine the will – they are determining only to the extent that *Willkür* allows them to be so. The other important point made here is that the choice of which incentives are to reign is not carried out in random fashion but in

---

61. See, e.g., *Religion*, p. 50n. (English, p. 45n.), where Kant explicitly espouses a kind of "determinism" (as opposed to "predeterminism") and declares that "freedom does not consist in the contingency (*Zufälligkeit*) of the act (that it is determined by no grounds whatsoever), i.e., in indeterminism."
62. *Religion*, pp. 23–4; English, p. 19.

accord with maxims, or general rules. Hence, Kant's conception of a subjective ground turns out to be nothing more than the notion of a maxim that played a central role in his earlier moral writings. A maxim, Kant tells us in the *Groundwork*, is the "subjective principle of willing" or, more clearly, the "principle in accord with which the subject acts."[63]

This distinction between a subjective and objective ground is relatively easy to grasp. What is less clear, is why invoking the notion of a subjective ground for *Willkür's* choices enables us to regard those choices as free. Why are acts that are determined by subjective grounds free, while those determined objectively are considered unfree? To this question Kant gives the following response: *Willkür's* choice of one incentive over its rival can be understood as free only if the adoption of the subjective ground which determines that choice is itself an "act of freedom."[64] In other words, *Willkür* chooses between two incentives on the basis of a maxim, but one can always then ask about the subject's choice of the maxim itself, and the problem of comprehending *Willkür's* freedom is simply pushed back one step from the level of choice between two particular acts to that of choosing between two (or more) general principles: Why does *Willkür* choose one maxim over its rival? Is this choice merely arbitrary, or does it too have a determining ground of some sort? Once again, Kant rejects the conclusion that its choices at this more general level are simply groundless or undetermined. At the same time, he realizes that if *Willkür* is to be a faculty of freedom, its acts of adopting maxims may not be traced back to a first *objective* ground – that is, they are not to be explained at any level as the result of determination by natural causes. Hence Kant opts for the same route he followed in the earlier case and maintains that the choice of a determining maxim must have its own subjective ground in yet another, presumably more general maxim. It then becomes clear, however, that this series of subjective grounds runs the risk of becoming an infinite regress that never arrives at a first, self-determined ground and that therefore fails to explain in what sense the choices determined by those grounds are "free."

As is well known, Kant's solution is to avoid an infinite regress by invoking the notion of a disposition (*Gesinnung*) in which all of

---

63. GMS, pp. 400n., 421n.
64. "Ein Aktus der Freiheit," *Religion*, p. 21; English, p. 17.

Willkür's particular choices are ultimately grounded. 'Disposition' here does not refer to empirical personality traits but rather to the most basic rule in accord with which a subject adopts all of its maxims. The distinction between a good and an evil disposition boils down simply to the question: Is the character of the individual such that she has made it a universal practice to subordinate all maxims unconditionally to the moral law? Now, if the disposition itself is to be a moral phenomenon – if we are to be able to describe it as good or evil – then it too must somehow be freely chosen by the person who possesses it. In fact, Kant regards the choice that constitutes one's moral disposition as simply another instance of the adoption of a maxim, although in this case the maxim at issue is the most general of all, namely, whether to make the moral law the guiding principle behind all of one's morally relevant deeds. Since the choice of one's fundamental disposition cannot be a fact given in experience, it must be thought of as the result of an "intelligible deed that precedes all experience."[65] The individual "earns" (*erwirbt*) her disposition, but only through a fundamental choice that must be regarded as taking place outside of all temporally conditioned experience.

Let us now take a step back from the details of Kant's account of free choice and attempt to articulate more precisely what is contained in the notion of freedom ascribed to *Willkür* and how all of this is relevant to the issue of self-determination. Willed actions within the empirical world are regarded as free because they are not causally determined but are instead the results of choices made by *Willkür* in accord with maxims. It is not the case, however, that in each of its choices the subject simply chooses its determining maxim from point zero. Practical maxims, rather, are chosen on the basis of more general principles, which themselves derive from even higher ones, all of which are ultimately grounded in the choice of the most basic principle of all, which Kant identifies with the choice of one's moral disposition. *Willkür*'s choices at the level of particular acts are free, then, not on the basis of some property that is intrinsic to each and independent of the rest of one's choices, but rather because they all depend upon a fundamental choice made by the subject in a realm outside of all experience. Kant's strategy, of course, requires that this original choice itself be an act of freedom, which in this case means that

65. *Religion*, p. 39n.; English, p. 34n.

the dispositional choice is not grounded in some higher principle but is in some sense "self-grounded." Since Kant provides no alternative explanation of the self-groundedness of this original choice, we can only conceive of it negatively, as spontaneous and ultimately arbitrary.

Finally, it is worth noting that on this view the freedom characteristic of *Willkür*'s particular choices can be understood as a kind of self-determination. The crucial point to recall here is that for Kant the distinction between a caused event and a freely chosen act is not identical to, or in any way dependent upon, the distinction one might make between a determined and an undetermined event. The difference, rather, turns upon the distinction between two different kinds of determining grounds (*Bestimmungsgründe*): objective and subjective. This is why Kant can say, as he does, that the acts chosen by *Willkür* are subject to a kind of determinism and, what is the same, that the notion of freedom that characterizes those acts is not equivalent to indeterminism.[66] Now, in order that the "determined" nature of free acts also be understood as constituting a kind of freedom, it is clear that the determination involved in these acts must be a species of *self*-determination. The free acts of *Willkür* are free not because they are undetermined or groundless, but because they are self-determined, where the term 'self-determined' means that my free choices are carried out in accord with maxims that themselves derive from a more general conception of my fundamental nature. What I choose to do is self-determined because it follows from "who I am," or from my most basic identity, an identity that is itself the result of my own (noumenal) choice. This notion of self-determination implied by Kant's account of *Willkür* is not to be confused with the conception of moral autonomy that is central to his moral philosophy, for, unlike the latter, it has no normative significance but is intended only to describe the sense in which free actions are free or self-grounded. In this sense, the actions of both evil and morally good agents are self-determined, since both kinds of maxims equally derive from one's fundamental moral disposition.

Having laid out the basic features of Kant's understanding of *Willkür*, we are now in a position to ask what motivated him to develop such a complex and counterintuitive view of human

---

66. *Religion*, p. 50n.; English, p. 45n.

choice. Why should one not be content with Reinhold's more straightforward view? In the first place, I believe that Kant preferred his account to Reinhold's because it implies that some form of general principle governs all empirical events, including both natural, objective processes and the willed action of human subjects. This is accomplished not by subsuming both classes of events under a single kind of "grounding" such as the principle of natural causality, but rather by using the notion of a subjective ground to articulate a second sense in which a particular class of empirical events, human actions, can be said to be determined. To say that some form of principle governs all empirical events implies that there is a sense in which all such events can be understood or explained, although the distinction between a subjective and an objective ground means that our way of understanding natural events will differ from that which applies to chosen deeds. The former are understood by locating their causes in a temporally prior state of affairs, while the latter are explained, at least in principle, by discerning the maxims that determine them and by understanding those principles as consistent with a most general maxim or, as Kant conceives it, with one's fundamental disposition. In other words, Kant's account of *Willkür* implies a view of human agency that is fundamentally different from that proposed by Reinhold. For Kant, the individual deeds of human agents are not to be understood as the results of so many random, unconnected acts of choice but are instead related to each other in the sense that they can all be understood as manifestations of a single, fundamental disposition.

It is clear from his own attempts to understand self-determination that Fichte rejects the account of self-determined choice just outlined. Nowhere does he explicitly lay out his reasons for this, but I believe it is possible to determine retrospectively what those reasons must have been. On the most general level, it is not that Kant's account is incoherent but rather that it fails to capture certain features essential to the phenomenon of self-determination. In the first place, and most obviously, Kant's theory fails to allow for the possibility of moral improvement or, more generally, for the possibility of development of one's basic character.[67] Since the

---

67. Kant himself recognizes and struggles with this problem in a variety of places: *Religion*, pp. 31, 37, 44, 47, 50; English, pp. 27, 32, 40, 43, 46.

choices one makes in the empirical world derive from one's fundamental disposition but do not have the capacity to affect or to amend that original choice, it is difficult to see how one's character could ever undergo genuine change.

The second reason for rejecting Kant's account constitutes, I believe, a more fundamental critique of that position and is more central to Fichte's own primary concerns as well. In very general terms, what Fichte must object to is Kant's use of a noumenal subject as a ground for the choices made by the practical subject in the empirical world. This wish to avoid recourse to a noumenal subject is, at least on Fichte's own self-understanding, closely connected to his conception of subjectivity in general, as it is articulated in the notion of a self-positing subject. This notion finds partial expression in such statements as "What does not exist for itself is not a subject," and "The subject exists only for itself."[68] What is intended here is a rejection of the view that the subjectively constituted aspects of experience, whether in self-determined action or in the theoretical constitution of the experienced world, are to be understood as the results of the activity of a subject that exists previous to and apart from all conscious experience. Although this view was originally developed by Fichte in the context of theoretical philosophy, it applies as well to the analysis of practical subjectivity. With respect to the specific issue of self-determination, it implies the rejection of Kant's notion of a fundamental choice that falls outside of all time and experience and that grounds all of one's particular choices. Hence, in the context of the issue of self-determination Fichte's wish to be rid of the noumenal subject converges with the common intuition that a theory in which the acts of an empirical agent are determined by the choice of a noumenal subject does not really provide us with an account of *self*-determination. From my perspective as an empirical subject, the original choice of my disposition is not my own in any meaningful sense, since it is something which necessarily takes place outside my own awareness and over which I have no control. From this point of view, my freely acquired disposition appears as an innate character so that what, from the noumenal perspective, is self-determination must appear to the empirical agent as just another mode of determination by something external to "me."

---

68. "Was für sich selbst nicht ist, ist kein Ich" (SW, I, p. 97); "das Ich [ist] nur für sich selbst" (SW, I, p. 457).

The task facing us now is to understand how Fichte can give an account of self-determination without resorting to the hypothesis of a noumenal subject, that is, solely in terms of the conscious subject's relation to itself. To do so, we must recall that Fichte's strategy was to conceive of substantive self-determination in terms of the subject's ability to reflect upon its "true essential nature." Furthermore, in the account under consideration here the subject's nature was to be understood as the nature of a particular individual rather than of subjects in general. Hence, we must first ask what it means for a practical subject, as an individual, to have a true nature. The answer Fichte gives to this question is closely related to his notion of self-positing subjectivity and, more particularly, to the way in which a subject differs from a thing. In a passage that strikingly anticipates themes within twentieth-century existentialism, Fichte locates the central difference between a subject and a thing in the contrasting senses in which each can be said to have a nature:

> A free being must exist before it is determined – it must have an existence which is independent of its determinacy. For this reason a thing cannot be thought as self-determining, because it does not exist prior to its nature, i.e., prior to the whole of its determinations. . . . A being that is to determine *itself* [however] would have to exist in a certain respect . . . before it has properties and a nature in general. This can be understood only on the presupposition that the free being exists, prior to its real existence, as an intelligence with the concept of its real existence and that the latter contains the ground of the former.[69]

For our purposes the important point of this passage is the claim that the essential nature of a free (or self-determining) being, unlike that of a thing, is not simply given along with the fact of its existence, but instead the being's essential nature follows from its concept of what it is. In the case of a self-determined agent, in other words, the conception within consciousness of one's essential identity precedes the real existence of that nature. In order to understand what this might mean more concretely, we should recall that in Kant's account of *Gesinnung* precisely the opposite is the case. There one's essential nature, as defined by the concept of moral disposition, is, from the perspective of the

69. SW, IV, p. 36.

empirical subject, already constituted prior to the particular choices made by *Willkür.* The choices I make in the empirical realm follow from my original ordering of fundamental values that is established by the dispositional choice. For Kant, then, there is a sense in which "who I am essentially," understood as the hierarchy of values to which I subscribe, precedes and determines my individual choices and deeds in the empirical world. In contrast to the view that Fichte is attempting to formulate, for Kant, my essential nature precedes my real existence.

Our problem now becomes one of understanding how Fichte can claim, on the one hand, that self-determination requires reflection upon one's true nature and, on the other hand, that one's true nature is not something that is merely found or given to the subject as already constituted but rather depends in some way upon the subject's own "concept" of itself. At this point it is necessary to recall Fichte's statement, cited earlier, concerning the distinctive nature of the subject's relation to itself, in contrast to the relation a subject has to an object in representational consciousness. The self-awareness at issue here (i.e., in practical self-determination) is a self-positing – or, as Fichte repeatedly says, it is more than a "passive looking on," more than a mere apprehending of an independent, already existing something. Rather, the subject's reflecting upon itself actually constitutes, in part, that which it apprehends.

Now, is there a way of making sense of this notion of reflection, according to which, in reflecting upon one's true nature, one allegedly constitutes that nature? At this point we must leave Fichte's texts behind, for they fail to provide a more determinate answer to this question. My suggestion, however, is that some help can be found by turning to a recent discussion of self-determination by Ernst Tugendhat.[70] According to Tugendhat, self-determination requires that the subject reflect upon its true nature in the sense of posing to itself what he calls the "fundamental practical question": Who am I really? Which among my manifold desires, intentions, and social roles represent the real me? For Tugendhat, as for Fichte, this question is not primarily a theoretical one to which an answer can be found simply through

---

70. *Self-Consciousness and Self-Determination,* cited earlier. Tugendhat himself understands his account of self-determination as a part of "the tradition following Fichte" (*die sich an Fichte anschließende Tradition*). A historical account of this tradition is found on pp. 132–43.

introspection. It is, rather, a question to which there is no already existing, fully determinate answer, a question that can be answered only by actually choosing what one's true nature is to be. To ask, "Who am I?" in a fundamental way, then, is really to ask "What kind of person do I want to be and how do I want to live my life?" To answer this question is not to "find" one's true self but to create, or to constitute, in part, one's basic identity. Furthermore, to reflect upon oneself at this fundamental level, and to make one's choices in accord with this reflection, is to escape heteronomous determination by immediate desires, conventional norms, or unexamined value commitments and, instead, to determine oneself.

Put another way, Tugendhat's account of self-determination can be understood as an attempt to develop Fichte's central, and controversial, claim concerning the self-constituting nature of reflection. The claim here is that the subject's reflection upon its essential identity opens up the possibility for a deeper kind of self-determination than that involved in Fichte's notion of merely "formal" freedom. Thus, on this view, reflection can accomplish more than simply allowing us to avoid being determined by our immediate desires and impulses; it can also enable us to escape determination by conventional, or "heteronomous," *norms*. In other words, the account of reflection that both Tugendhat and Fichte espouse will involve something more than merely *employing* socially derived norms and conventions to determine which of one's desires are worthy of being acted upon. Their view asserts, rather, that norms can in some sense actually be *constituted* for us within the process of reflection and that such constitution of norms is what self-determination at its deepest level consists in.

This view raises an obvious but important question: What is the nature of that process by means of which the subject comes to espouse its most fundamental values? Do I simply choose my identity arbitrarily? Is my adoption of basic norms wholly, or even in part, based upon some kind of reasoning? Or are my fundamental choices ultimately determined "from without" by unexamined, perhaps unconscious norms that I inherit from my culture or social class? Let us consider these three possibilities more systematically. First, if the adoption of one's fundamental principles is spontaneous in the sense of being wholly ungrounded, then an obvious objection arises, one that is reminiscent of Kant's critique of Reinhold's conception of the nature of the spontaneity involved in particular free acts: If my choice of principles is truly un-grounded, and therefore cannot be explained as following from a reason or from some basic feature of myself, such as my character, then in what meaningful sense are they "my own"? In this case, the notion of completely arbitrary choice, already rejected at the level of individual deeds, simply recurs at a much higher level where the object of my choice is my fundamental identity. Yet the second possibility – the view that these highest values are chosen rationally – seems no more promising. For if rational choice makes sense only in the context of higher principles to which one is already committed, then principles that are the products of rational choice depend upon even higher-level commitments, about which a theory of self-determination must ask: Are *they* the subject's own? And, if so, in what sense? It is obvious that continuing in this way one can never reach a principle that is both highest and rationally grounded. This conclusion leads us to the third possi-bility suggested above, namely, that one's most basic value com-mitments ultimately derive not from oneself, but from the various social groups to which one belongs, so that one's basic identity is essentially a product of one's social formation. It would seem, then, that we are left with the following conclusion: One's highest, seemingly self-determined values are in reality determined either by a choice that is thoroughly arbitrary, or externally by inherited social norms. But in either case the notion of self-determination seems to be illusory.

Is there a way out of this dilemma that takes cognizance of these objections and still is capable of defending a substantive concep-tion of self-determination? Although Tugendhat is not unaware of this problem, he fails in the end to provide a wholly satisfactory solution to it. This is due in part to two related assumptions he makes about the nature of self-determination, namely, that what is at issue in self-determination is the choice of one's *deepest* values, and that in order to be considered self-determined in a substantive sense, the choice of those values must be made from a position that abstracts from all established, pregiven norms. This last assumption, however, falls prey to the argument that has been made in criticism of theories of radical autonomy (including Tugendhat's) – that the individual is unable to choose his identity in any meaningful way from a perspective that is completely void of *all* preexisting value commitments.[71] (We shall set aside for now

71. See, e.g., Larmore (1987, pp. 92–6, and throughout).

the further question of the *desirability* of striving to attain such a perspective.) Not only is it a fact of human development that we arrive at the age of maturity with already constituted systems of value, but it is also conceptually problematic to suggest that one can simply determine what is ultimately valuable in abstraction from all other values. In other words, we must abandon Tugendhat's notion that to be self-determined in a substantive sense one must stand back from all pregiven norms in order to choose the most basic principles according to which one wants to live one's life.

If we grant this point, however, are we thereby committed to abandoning the very concept of substantive self-determination, or is there a weaker sense of this notion that can still be defended? This question is perhaps best addressed by considering a concrete example of the kind of self-determined choice that Tugendhat seems to have in mind: A young woman faces the decision of whether to marry a certain man whom she loves but who has deeply rooted, traditional ideas concerning marriage, family life, and the roles of men and women in each. A sober assessment of her future tells the woman that each of the two alternatives offers real but contrasting goods. One life offers the possibility of a greater degree of personal independence, the chance to pursue a career, perhaps more risk and adventure, while the other offers the rewards of parenting, stability, and a life together with a man whom, after all, she is in love with. In order to choose in a self-determined mode the woman must realize that the decision she faces involves more than the choice between two particular actions; it is also a choice between two distinct identities. In posing the questions "Who am I? Which of the two lives is really me?" she asks herself not a factual question about her identity, but a fundamental practical question about the relative values of distinct and incommensurable goods. The point I take to be implicit in Tugendhat's (and Fichte's) view of the practical subject is that it would be mistaken to suppose that the woman had at her disposal an already established hierarchy of values that she must simply consult in order to decide whether to marry. Rather, her decision, if self-determined, must proceed from a ranking of values that emerges only in the process of reflecting upon the kind of person she wants to be.[72]

---

72. It should be noted that this is not the *only* scenario on which the decision to marry would count as self-determined. For the decision might also follow

Before we go on to consider whether this example allows us to make sense of some weaker notion of self-determination, it is important to call attention to a crucial point that Tugendhat hints at but does not adequately emphasize, namely, that self-determination, posing to oneself the fundamental practical question, is to be understood as inherently situational.[73] One does not ask about one's true identity simply as a matter of course, but only in rather special circumstances. What this means, I believe, is that "who I really am" becomes an issue for me only when my system of values "breaks down," that is, only when I realize that the values according to which I have lived until now are insufficient to inform a life that I can recognize as satisfying. This realization can occur in a variety of circumstances: when my beliefs about myself or the world undergo significant change (e.g., I come to see that my closest personal relationships have been based upon self-deception); when I find that two of my values conflict in a fundamental way (my wish to develop my artistic talents vs. a desire to become a political activist); or when, as in the present example, the relations among my previous commitments are insufficiently determinate to tell me what to do in the particular situation I face.

None of these cases requires the individual involved to abstract from *all* of her value commitments but, more accurately, to harmonize a certain subset of those values – the ones at issue in the particular situation – both with each other and with what one knows (or believes) to be the case. Thus, in the present example, the woman does not set aside all of her normative commitments; in fact, she does not even set aside those that her situation calls into question, for she does not ask simply, "Should I value independence (or, alternatively, a domestic existence)?" but rather, "When these two values conflict, which of them should I deem to be more important?" Of course, the suggestion that self-determination consists in harmonizing the different values to which one subscribes must not be taken to mean that it is only, or even primarily, a matter of infusing them with mere logical consistency.

---

from an already constituted disposition that was itself the result of a previous, fully reflective choice. Since the intelligibility of this possibility, however, relies upon our ability to make sense of the notion of self-constituting reflection, only the latter need be considered in detail here.

73. See Tugendhat (1986, p. 172), where he characterizes the fundamental practical question as always "situationally related" (*situationsbezogen*) but fails to draw from this the conclusions I suggest here.

For it is often the case that what are *logically* consistent values in the abstract become, in the context of real-life situations, *practically* incompatible. Furthermore, although the agent in such situations certainly possesses "higher" (i.e., more general and more firmly held) practical principles (e.g., that it is wrong to take innocent lives), it need not be the case that these principles suffice to settle the particular conflict of values at issue. Hence, the "harmonizing" of one's normative commitments in this view of self-determination involves determining which of two distinct values is to be preferred over the other in the absence of any already existing principle that could resolve the conflict.

But how is such "self-determination" – the determination of the relative worth of one's values – to proceed? One way of conceptualizing something very close to this weaker sense of substantive self-determination has been suggested by Charles Taylor.[74] On his account, determining for oneself what one really values is to be understood not in terms of a *choice* that is made either of or among values, but rather as a process of *articulating* more explicitly and with greater clarity one's original, "inchoate" sense of what is worthy. In other words, the agent who is faced with having to decide which values he will live by does not attempt to choose among possible values but undertakes instead a search within, a reflection upon his "deepest unstructured sense of what is important" with the aim of formulating and defining that original sense in clearer, more precisely articulated terms. But if this is how one's normative questions are settled, in what sense can this process be termed "self-determination"? It seems on this scenario that the subject, rather than *constituting* its evaluations, engages in something like a theoretical enterprise to *discern* what it truly holds to be important. Taylor agrees with this characterization in part, for he believes that it is possible for one self-interpretation to be more or less "adequate" (i.e., more or less *true*) than another. But at the same time he denies that reflection upon one's values can be understood as just a species of theoretical inquiry, for he holds that in articulating my values I also constitute them, at least in part. To articulate one's sense of what is worthy is not merely to describe or define an independently constituted object but actually

74. Taylor (1983, pp. 118–26). Although Taylor does not use the term 'self-determination', he treats the same issue in his discussion of the agent's responsibility for its "strong evaluations."

"to make it something different from what it was before."[75] Taylor's position here has a deep affinity with Fichte's theory of subjectivity, for what he suggests is simply a version of the thesis of the self-positing subject: In reflecting upon itself the subject also constitutes itself. Taylor's attempt to characterize the kind of reflection involved in determining what one holds to be of value is provocative, but it never quite succeeds in answering the question of central importance: In what sense is my articulation of my values to be understood as also constituting those values, beyond the obvious sense that what is originally implicit and vague becomes explicit and more defined?

A second possibility for understanding substantive self-determination in a weaker sense is suggested by modifying the account of Tugendhat's described earlier. Here the basic point to be gleaned from Tugendhat is the idea that when faced with a "breakdown" in one's system of values, the self-determining individual has more at her disposal than merely arbitrary "picking" but somewhat less than the wholly determined rational choice characterized earlier. The reason this choice cannot be "fully" rational (in the sense of being completely determined by reasons) is that, as suggested before, although the individual is not completely without prior normative commitments, she does not necessarily possess a fully articulated hierarchy of values that specifies the relation that is to hold between values that come into conflict. On Tugendhat's view, the self-determining subject attempts to resolve its dilemma by searching for reasons to choose one norm over another, but it is seldom the case that such reasons completely determine the decision's outcome.[76] At some point, having carried out the search for rational justification as far as possible, I am left simply to make my choice.

It will no doubt be objected that on this scenario the decision that is made rests upon what is ultimately an arbitrary choice. But is this conclusion justified? Let us suppose that for the woman in our example the prospect of individual autonomy wins out over

75. Taylor (1983, p. 123).
76. Tugendhat (1986) suggests a variety of ways in which reasoning plays a role in self-determination. Included are a realistic assessment of one's available options; the individual's self-knowledge, i.e., knowledge of one's dispositions, capabilities, motives, etc.; an evaluation of the truth of one's beliefs about what constitutes well-being; and "moral" reasoning about the legitimate claims of others upon my action. See pp. 214, 313.

the attractions of family life. It would surely not be right to regard this choice of *a course of action* (i.e., to break off the relationship) as merely arbitrary. If asked, the woman could even provide a reason for choosing as she did: "I chose to remain single because of the independence it offers me." What is distinctive about her situation, however, is that the principle embodied in her choice – that individual autonomy is more important than the rewards of establishing a family – did not exist for her prior to the particular choice itself. What the analysis of substantive self-determination is really concerned with, then, is her espousal of a value – her decision to let one reason (her independence) count as decisive with respect to another (family life). As suggested earlier, I believe it would be wrong to say that one value was chosen on the basis of a higher principle that was already a part of the woman's set of normative commitments. Yet it seems equally wrong to say that her opting for independence is merely arbitrary or blind, for the choice follows a process of deep reflection and reasoning about what is best (a process that certainly may involve an appeal to other, unquestioned values), even if the reasons produced by such a process are ultimately insufficient to determine the choice. If some sense is to be made, then, of the notion of substantive self-determination, it seems that it is here that one must look, namely, in the agent's capacity, in situations where his values conflict, not merely to determine which action to take in this particular situation but to establish for himself a normative *principle* (e.g., that one value is more important than another), according to which this choice is made. While it is true that such an espousal of norms might be regarded as "ungrounded" in a strict sense of that term, it is also more than merely "blind." For, apart from the important fact that this kind of self-determination involves a search for rational justification, the choices that result from it are ones about which the subject possesses a significant kind of self-transparency. In opting to pursue one value over another I do so with a clear awareness both of what is at stake for me in the decision, as well as of the limits to the reasons I have for choosing as I do.

In light of the qualifications that have been made here of the notion of self-determination, one might well ask whether it is still reasonable to call what has been described "self-determination." To put the question in Fichtean terms, in what sense does this account of the practical subject's reflection upon itself involve a "self-positing," or in what sense does this subject constitute itself

or determine its identity? As we saw earlier, one of the requirements for a theory of substantive self-determination is that it
explain how the practical subject can give to itself maxims for its
action that do not simply follow logically from higher-level principles that are already given. But if the practical subject is to determine for itself *maxims,* or *principles* of action, it must view the result
of its reflection as the adoption of a value rather than as merely a
choice of a particular action. That is, it must see itself as deciding
to live a life in which one value is consistently (though not necessarily universally) subordinated to another. In what sense is this
true of the account just given? That is, why should we regard the
woman as constituting for herself a normative *principle* rather than
merely choosing one particular action over another in a situation
where her established normative commitments are insufficient to
decide the case?

There are two ways of answering this question: The first focuses
on an objective feature of the action chosen, while the second
refers to a subjective quality of the agent itself. An important
feature of the examples to which this (and Tugendhat's) account
of self-determination typically appeal is that they are instances in
which what is to be chosen is a "form of life" rather than merely
an isolated deed. What one chooses in such cases is not a single
action, but an objectively realized way of life that consistently
requires the subordination of one value to another and that, once
entered into, is not easily abandoned or exchanged. To opt, for
example, for the monastic life is not simply to choose a particular
action but to espouse instead a form of life, the objective features
of which necessitate that one value (e.g., sensual pleasure) be
regularly subordinated to another (e.g., contemplation). Making
this kind of fundamental commitment is, in a very straightforward
sense, to choose for oneself the kind of person one wants to be. But
surely it is not only in cases where my choice objectively binds me
to a particular form of life that one can speak of the choice of principles, and hence of substantive self-determination. For deciding
to act can involve more than the choice of a single deed when the
agent also resolves to regard the choice as embodying a rule that
is to be followed consistently. At least in some cases, the very
process of engaging in serious deliberation, of posing "fundamental practical questions" to oneself, results not only in the
decision to take a particular course of action, but also in a (subjective) commitment to the value embodied in the choice, a commit-

ment to resolve future conflicts in favor of the same set of values that won out in the earlier case.[77]

At this point one might ask whether such a weakened account of self-determination can still be recognized as Fichtean or, more accurately, as inspired by his second, "individualist" conception of substantive self-determination that was laid out previously. We have already noted one way in which the account just suggested embodies a weaker version of self-determination than the one envisioned by Fichte. For the former denies the claim, implicit in Fichte's account, that the self-determining subject constructs for itself a single hierarchy of values, at the top of which resides a highest, inviolable principle. On the view offered here, self-determination also consists in instilling one's values with a kind of hierarchy, but it is a hierarchy that is only partial and not necessarily subsumed under one supreme maxim.

Closely related to this point is another, perhaps more important sense in which this vision of self-determination is weaker than Fichte's: On our account the practical subject that reflects upon "its true nature" is no longer conceived as "pure," or stripped of *all* of its normative commitments. What this implies, as I have said, is that the notion of *radical* self-determination – where the subject is regarded as the sole source of its deepest values – is to be abandoned. Although this qualification runs counter to what is usually taken to be the main thrust of Fichte's ethical thought, it is also possible to see this rejection of radical self-determination as the kernel of truth in Fichte's well-known dictum that the ideal of self-determination is "an unattainable goal, but one which [the subject], in accord with its spiritual nature, ought unceasingly to approach."[78] Yet even here Fichte seems to regard self-determination as an unqualifiedly desirable ideal, one to be pursued "unceasingly" and, presumably, regardless of one's circumstances. On our account, however, the self-determined, critical examination of one's value commitments need not – indeed, cannot – be a continuous activity, for the kind of determination of one's values characterized here is occasioned only by situations, themselves mostly beyond the individual's control, in which one's given system of values is shown to be inadequate as a guide for action.

---

77. This point is suggested and discussed more fully by Nozick (1981, pp. 297, 305–6).
78. SW, IV, p. 149; see also pp. 66, 229.

The intuition behind Fichte's position that it is the I's vocation to strive for self-determination must be that the practical subject operates as a rational agent in the deepest sense, not when it deliberates only about what particular acts to undertake, but when it submits the very standards according to which it lives to critical examination. I believe that there is an important truth in this general assertion but that Fichte's notion of substantive self-determination misconceives the way in which the subject's examination of its values must take place. For the claim implicit in Fichte's position is that it is possible to understand one's espousal of values as "self-determination" in a strong sense, one that requires these norms to be evaluated in accord with one's highest principles, which themselves are ultimately self-given. I have argued, however, that something like this scenario arises only in situations where one is faced with a conflict between distinct values for which one does not already have a higher-level principle to decide the case, and that what is self-given in such cases is not the values themselves, nor some "highest" maxim, but something more modest – a principle that ranks one given value with respect to another. What is to be rejected, then, is the idea, central to Fichte's account, that the subject's practical standards can all be ultimately *self-given*, as well as the illusion, already contained in Kant's theory of moral disposition, upon which this idea is based, namely, that the subject is somehow capable of choosing itself at the deepest level of its identity.

CONCLUSION

In the preceding four chapters we have tried to understand Fichte's theory of subjectivity as one version of the general project of demonstrating the unity of theoretical and practical reason. After a survey of his early philosophical development, we arrived at the conclusion that by 1797 Fichte had come to regard his first principle of philosophy, as it is formulated in the thesis of the self-positing subject, as an attempt to grasp the essence of subjectivity in all of its configurations, or, what is the same, to articulate the single fundamental structure, or "activity," that underlies and informs all of consciousness. If this thesis is correct, then it must be possible to show that subjectivity in both its practical and theoretical forms depends upon an activity of the subject that has the structure of what Fichte calls "self-positing" activity. Our analysis of the notion of self-positing began in Chapter 3 with an examination of the issue in connection with which Fichte initially constructed his theory of subjectivity, namely, the phenomenon of theoretical self-consciousness. We saw there that Fichte's account of the subject as a self-positing activity, or *Tathandlung*, could be understood as a development of Kant's own view of the theoretical subject, especially with respect to two issues: the distinctive nature of the subject's self-awareness in theoretical self-consciousness and the absolute, or self-constituting, nature of the representing subject.

Starting with an account of the self-relation involved in theoretical self-consciousness, and with a firm commitment to the view that subjectivity must be essentially unitary, Fichte was led to the idea that practical subjectivity must also be regarded as grounded in an analogous kind of relation of the subject to itself. In this sphere Fichte's specific goal was described as isolating the fundamental characteristic of free human agency and then showing that this characteristic also depends upon a subjective activity that has the structure of self-positing. The feature of the subject that Fichte singled out here as essential to free agency was that of "self-determination." On this view, being a free agent, as opposed to a determined link in a causal chain, consists in determining one's actions oneself, rather than being determined to act by external causes. Furthermore, to be free in the deepest sense was said to require a self-determination, not only of one's particular deeds, but of the general principles according to which one lives one's life. It was primarily here – in the subject's adoption of its highest practical principles – that Fichte attempted to show that self-positing was necessary for practical subjectivity. He envisioned one's self-determined norms as arising only from an activity in which the subject enters into a uniquely "subjective" relation to itself, insofar as it reflects upon its essential nature and in the process constitutes its identity.

Thus far we have been concerned primarily with Fichte's separate accounts of theoretical and practical subjectivity (in Chapters 3 and 4, respectively) and, more specifically, with understanding how the central phenomena of the theoretical and practical realms could each be conceived of as dependent upon a self-positing activity. It now remains for us to consider briefly whether Fichte has succeeded at his task – to what extent do his discussions of self-consciousness and self-determination show that both forms of subjectivity are grounded in a *single* activity or, more accurately, in activities that have a truly identical structure?

The plausibility of Fichte's thesis lies in the fact that his accounts of the basic phenomena of theoretical and practical subjectivity both depend upon what one might call acts of "reflexive self-constitution." Contained in this notion is the idea that, in distinction to things, the subject *constitutes itself*, and it does so by entering into a distinctively "subjective" *self-relation* that differs from the relations (whether practical or theoretical) that a subject has to an object. This is the case in theoretical self-consciousness, insofar as a kind of reflexive, nonrepresentational activity (the I's relating its representations to itself) constitutes the subject with respect to its existence. Similarly, in the practical realm the subject is said to constitute itself – establish its own identity – through a kind of nonobjective self-relating. For, as a self-determining being, I determine the principles that will govern my actions by choosing them in accord with my conception of "who I am," where the identity that governs the choice of principles does not itself (fully) preexist the act of choosing but emerges instead only in the process of self-reflection.

It is important to note, however, that to demonstrate that theoretical and practical subjectivity share this one essential feature is not necessarily to show that they are structurally *identical*. One obvious, but significant difference between the two resides in the nature of the self-relation involved in each. In his account of theoretical self-consciousness, Fichte emphasizes that the subject's relation to itself is "immediate," which, as we saw earlier, is associated with the claim that the theoretical subject's most basic kind of awareness is implicit, involuntary, and prereflective. Yet none of these attributes applies to the self-relation that is central to practical self-determination. On the contrary, the kind of reflexive activity characteristic of this notion is a voluntary and explicit reflection upon one's "true essential nature" in which the subject even has itself as a kind of object for reflection. The self-relation involved here is still distinct from the subject's relations to objects, since the "object" of practical reflection is constituted through the act of reflecting, but it is also significantly different from the kind of immediate self-relation upon which theoretical self-consciousness depends.

There exists an even more basic difference between the two forms of subjectivity as Fichte understands them. It is a difference that Fichte himself seems not to have been aware of but that concerns one of the most fundamental aspects of his theory, the self-constituting nature of the subject. A careful consideration of Fichte's accounts of self-consciousness and self-determination reveals that there is an important asymmetry between the ways in which the subject constitutes itself in its theoretical and practical activities. We can best understand this difference by pointing out a basic ambiguity in the notion of self-constitution. On the one hand, an entity might be thought of as self-constituting with respect to its *existence,* so that the very fact that it exists is in some sense its own doing. On the other hand, a being might be said to constitute itself in a *qualitative* sense. Here it is not *that* I exist that is up to me but *how* I exist; the set of properties that make up my identity – the *kind* of being I am – depends, whether in toto or in part, upon my making myself thus. Having made this distinction, it is easy to see that Fichte conceives of the subject of theoretical self-consciousness as self-constituting in the first of these senses and attributes the second kind of self-constitution to the practical I. In the former case Fichte regards the subject as constituting itself with regard to its existence in the sense that in the absence of its self-positing activity – its immediate intuition of its representations as its own – the subject cannot be said to exist. In practical self-determination, however, it is not one's existence that is constituted through the subject's reflective activity; rather, the subject constitutes itself qualitatively – it determines what kind of a person it will be.

Although Fichte's theory draws our attention to the existence of important parallels between theoretical and practical subjectivity, the differences between them suggest that there are limits to the extent to which a clarification of the structure of theoretical self-consciousness can shed light on the nature of practical self-determination. Despite Fichte's inability to show that the two are informed by an *identical* structure, his basic thesis concerning the essentially unitary nature of subjectivity exerts a significant influence on subsequent philosophy. Most notably, not only does Hegel incorporate specifically Fichtean views concerning the self-positing nature of the subject into his notion of *Geist*, he also follows Fichte's lead in a more fundamental way by making his own conception of subjectivity (a subjectivity that, in a more basic sense than Fichte's I, is also essentially "other-relating") the first principle of philosophy. And, in a sense, Hegel carries Fichte's project one step farther, for he regards this transformed Fichtean principle as articulating not only the nature of human subjectivity but the structure of all reality.

These broader systematic issues aside, Fichte's theory has had a significant influence in at least two other areas. As we saw in Chapter 3, his view of theoretical self-consciousness, minus its transcendental claims, is probably the most important forerunner of twentieth-century phenomenological accounts, especially in Husserl and Sartre, of the nature of self-awareness and consciousness in general. But perhaps the most provocative and influential aspect of Fichte's theory lies in his view that practical self-determination can be understood only on the basis of a distinctive relation of the subject to itself, as well as in his attempt to articulate the nature of that self-relation. The view that human freedom in its most substantial form – that is, as self-determination or autonomy – is grounded in a distinctively subjective self-relating reappears in a variety of guises, not only in the thought of his Continental successors, but in some Anglo-American discussions of the topic as well.[1] In this respect, Fichte's theory makes an important contribution to one of philosophy's most important tasks, that of understanding how, and in what sense, human beings can be free.

1. For a detailed account of the forms this basic idea takes in Hegel, Kierkegaard, and Heidegger, see Tugendhat (1986, Chaps. 7, 10).

BIBLIOGRAPHY

Allison, Henry. *Kant's Transcendental Idealism: An Interpretation and Defense.* New Haven, Conn.: Yale Univ. Press, 1983.

Baumanns, Peter. *Fichtes ursprüngliches System: Sein Standort zwischen Kant und Hegel.* Stuttgart-Bad Cannstatt: Frommann-Holzboog, 1972.

Fichtes Wissenschaftslehre. Bonn: Bouvier, 1974.

Beiser, Frederick C. *The Fate of Reason: German Philosophy from Kant to Fichte.* Cambridge, Mass.: Harvard Univ. Press, 1987.

Benson, Robert Lawrence. "Fichte's Original Argument." Doctoral dissertation, Columbia Univ., 1974.

Breazeale, Daniel. "Between Kant and Fichte: Karl Leonhard Reinhold's 'Elementary Philosophy.' " *Review of Metaphysics,* 35 (1982), 785–822.

"Fichte's *Aenesidemus* Review and the Transformation of German Idealism." *Review of Metaphysics,* 34 (1981), 545–68.

"How to Make an Idealist: Fichte's 'Refutation of Dogmatism' and the Problem of the Starting Point of the *Wissenschaftslehre.* " *Philosophical Forum,* 19, Nos. 2–3 (1988), 97–123.

Ebbinghaus, Julius. "Fichtes ursprüngliche Philosophie." In *Gesammelte Aufsätze, Vorträge, und Reden.* Hildesheim: Olms, 1968, pp. 211–25.

Ferry, Luc. *Le droit: La nouvelle querelle des anciens et des modernes.* Vol. 1 of *Philosophie politique.* Paris: Presses universitaires de France, 1984.

Le système des philosophies de l'histoire. Vol. 2 of *Philosophie politique.* Paris: Presses universitaires de France, 1984.

Fichte, Immanuel H. *Johann Gottlieb Fichtes Leben und literarischer Briefwech-sel*, 2 vols. 1830; rpt. Leipzig: Brockhaus, 1862.

Fichte, Johann Gottlieb. *J. G. Fichte: Gesamtausgabe der Bayerischen Akademie der Wissenschaften*, 15 vols. Ed. Reinhard Lauth, Hans Jacobs, and Hans Gliwitsky. Stuttgart-Bad Cannstatt: Frommann-Holzboog, 1964– .

Johann Gottlieb Fichtes sämmtliche Werke, 8 vols. Ed. I. H. Fichte. Berlin: Veit & Comp., 1845–6.

Wissenschaftslehre nova methodo: Kollegnachschrift K. Chr. Fr. Krause 1798/ 1799. Ed. Erich Fuchs. Hamburg: Meiner, 1982.

Attempt at a Critique of All Revelation. Trans. Garrett Green. Cambridge Univ. Press, 1978.

Fichte: Early Philosophical Writings. Trans. Daniel Breazeale. Ithaca, N.Y.: Cornell Univ. Press, 1988.

The Science of Knowledge with the First and Second Introductions. Trans. Peter Heath and John Lachs. Cambridge Univ. Press, 1982.

The Vocation of Man. Ed. Roderick M. Chisholm. Indianapolis, Ind.: Bobbs-Merrill, 1956.

Frank, Manfred. *Die Unhintergehbarkeit von Individualität: Reflexionen über Subjekt, Person und Individuum aus Anlaß ihrer "postmodernen" Toter-klärung*. Frankfurt am Main: Suhrkamp, 1986.

Heimsoeth, Heinz. *Fichte*. Munich: E. Reinhardt, 1923.

Henrich, Dieter. "Der Begriff der sittlichen Einsicht und Kants Lehre vom Faktum der Vernunft." In *Die Gegenwart der Griechen im neueren Denken*. Ed. D. Henrich, W. Schulz, and K.-H. Volkmann-Schluck. Tübingen: Mohr, 1960, 77–115.

"La découverte de Fichte." *Revue de metaphysique et de morale*, 72 (1967) 154–69.

"Fichte's ursprüngliche Einsicht." In *Subjektivität und Metaphysik*. Ed. D. Henrich and H. Wagner. Frankfurt am Main: Klostermann, 1966, 188–232.

Selbstverhältnisse. Stuttgart: Reclam, 1982.

"Ueber die Einheit der Subjektivität." *Philosophische Rundschau*, 3 (1955), 28–69.

"Fichte's Original Insight." Trans. David R. Lachterman. *Contempo-rary German Philosophy* I. University Park, Pa.: Pennsylvania State Univ. Press, 1982, 15–53.

"Self-Consciousness: A Critical Introduction to a Theory." *Man and World*, 4 (1971), 3–28.

Kabitz, Willy. *Studien zur Entwicklungsgeschichte der Fichteschen Wissenschafts-lehre aus der Kantischen Philosophie*. 1902; rpt. Darmstadt: Wis-senschaftliche Buchgesellschaft, 1968.

Kant, Immanuel. *Gesammelte Schriften, Akademie-Ausgabe*, 32 vols. Berlin: Reimer, 1902–83.

Critique of Judgment. Trans. J. H. Bernard. New York: Macmillan, 1951.
Critique of Practical Reason. Trans. L. W. Beck. Indianapolis, Ind.: Bobbs-Merrill, 1956.
Critique of Pure Reason. Trans. Norman Kemp Smith. 1929; rpt. New York: St. Martin's, 1965.
Groundwork of the Metaphysic of Morals. Trans. H. J. Paton. New York: Harper & Row, 1964.
Religion Within the Bounds of Reason Alone. Trans. Theodore M. Greene and Hoyt H. Hudson. 1934; rpt. New York: Harper, 1960.
Larmore, Charles E. *Patterns of Moral Complexity.* Cambridge Univ. Press, 1987.
Lauth, Reinhard. "J. G. Fichtes Gesamtidee der Philosophie." *Philosophisches Jahrbuch,* 71 (1964), 253–85.
Léon, Xavier. *Fichte et son temps,* 3 vols. 1914; rpt. Paris: Armand Colin, 1954.
Nozick, Robert. *Philosophical Explanations.* Cambridge, Mass.: Harvard Univ. Press, 1981.
Paton, H. J. *The Categorical Imperative: A Study in Kant's Moral Philosophy.* Philadelphia: Univ. of Pennsylvania Press, 1971.
Perrinjaquet, Alain. "La conscience de soi comme point de départ de la philosophie dans la deuxième exposition de la doctrine de la science de J. G. Fichte." Mémoire présenté pour l'obtention de la licence ès lettres. Univ. de Neuchâtel, 1985.
Philonenko, Alexis. *La liberté humaine dans la philosophie de Fichte.* Paris: Vrin, 1966.
Théorie et praxis dans la pensée morale et politique de Kant et de Fichte de 1793. Paris: Vrin, 1968.
Pippin, Robert B. "Fichte's Contribution." *Philosophical Forum,* 19, Nos. 2–3 (1988), 74–96.
Hegel's Idealism: The Satisfactions of Self-Consciousness. Cambridge Univ. Press, 1989.
Reinhold, Karl Leonhard. *Beiträge zur Berichtigung bisheriger Mißverständnisse der Philosophen*, Vol. 1. Jena: Mauke, 1790.
Briefe über die Kantische Philosophie, Vol. 2. Leipzig: Goeschen, 1792.
Versuch einer neuen Theorie des menschlichen Vorstellungs-Vermögens. Prague: Widtmann & Mauke, 1789.
Renaut, Alain. *Le système du droit: Philosophie et droit dans la pensée de Fichte.* Paris: Presses universitaires de France, 1986.
Sartre, Jean-Paul. *Being and Nothingness.* Trans. Hazel E. Barnes. New York: Pocket Books, 1966.
The Transcendence of the Ego. Trans. Forrest Williams and Robert Kirkpatrick. New York: Noonday Press, 1957.
Schulze, Gottlob Ernst. *Aenesidemus oder über die Fundamente der von dem Herrn Professor Reinhold in Jena gelieferten Elementar-Philosophie.* 1792; rpt. Berlin: Reuther & Reichard, 1911.

Silber, John. "The Ethical Significance of Kant's *Religion.*" In *Religion Within the Bounds of Reason Alone.* Trans. Theodore M. Greene and Hoyt H. Hudson. 1934; rpt. New York: Harper, 1960, pp. lxxix–cxxxiv.

Siep, Ludwig. *Hegels Fichtekritik und die Wissenschaftslehre von 1804.* Freiburg: Alber, 1970.

Taylor, Charles. *Philosophical Papers.* Cambridge Univ. Press, 1985.

"Responsibility for Self." In *Free Will.* Ed. Gary Watson. New York: Oxford Univ. Press, 1983, pp. 111–26.

Tugendhat, Ernst. *Self-Consciousness and Self-Determination.* Trans. Paul Stern. Cambridge, Mass.: MIT Press, 1986.

Wildt, Andreas. *Autonomie und Anerkennung.* Stuttgart: Klett-Cotta, 1982.

INDEX

177

Printed in the United Kingdom
by Lightning Source UK Ltd.
9614400001B